Living in the Freedom of the Spirit

Tom Marshall

Sovereign World

Sovereign World Ltd
PO Box 777
Tonbridge
Kent TN11 0ZS
England

ISBN 1 85240 292 X

Typeset by CRB Associates, Reepham, Norfolk.
Printed in the United States of America.

Dedication

To Gabriele –
my loving and devoted wife with whom
it was such a joy to share the last few years
of my life and ministry in the gospel.

Contents

Foreword

Tom Marshall's contribution to Christian life and thought is almost a legend in our nation (New Zealand). He was one of the most valued, creative and sensitive thinkers in ministry I have ever known. *Living in the Freedom of the Spirit* is not only a practical and perceptive guide to wholeness in our lives, it is also a statement of the reality of Tom's own life and of what has happened so often to people helped by his ministry.

I am so grateful for the wisdom in this book, which like salvation is freely given, but was 'bought with a price'.

Winkie Pratney

Introduction

After a convention meeting one night I shared some of the insights from this book with a woman as an answer to her problems. With a stub of chalk I drew some of the diagrams on the blackboard as we stood in the half-dark hall.

Some weeks later she sent me a letter. 'I feel', she wrote, 'as if God has given me back a whole chunk of personality that I thought I had lost forever.' To me that speaks of the very essence of salvation; for Bible salvation is nothing short of the recovery of wholeness.

People are thinking, feeling, willing beings. That is to say, our basic nature consists of cognition (mind), affections (emotions) and volition (will). Together these constitute a living soul. Human beings also have a body, relating us to the external world, and we have a spirit, through which we can relate to the spiritual realm and to God. We are thus tripartite beings – spirit, soul and body (1 Thessalonians 5:23).

God is concerned with the whole person. It would be difficult to overemphasize this point. Many of our problems come from the mistaken idea that in salvation God rescues one part of us – our spirit – from general ruin, and abandons the rest. Nothing is further from the truth. God has always dealt with the whole person. We are to love the Lord our God with all our heart and all our soul and all our mind and all our strength. Sin has radically affected not only our spirit, but our mind, our will, and our emotions. But the wonderful news is that redemption reaches and recovers all those areas that sin has ruined.

Because we have not clearly understood this, many of us have the idea that to 'walk in the Spirit' we have to ignore, or suppress, or at best put up with, these other parts of our personality. They seem encumbrances we would be better off without. But they are still there, even if we try to pretend otherwise. We still have feelings, we still have a mind and so on. If these areas are not redeemed and open to the Lord, there is only one other direction in which they can be open: towards the world, the flesh and the devil. Then we wonder why Christians get depressed, or have trouble with compulsive thoughts, or can't break free from old habits.

Jesus always looked for a total response from those who would be His disciples. In the gospels, it sometimes appears that the Lord checked people out in the area of mind, emotions and will. If He found the response defective in one of other of these areas, He went to some trouble to put it right.

In Matthew chapter 8 a scribe came to Jesus and said, *'Teacher, I will follow you wherever you go.'* Instead of welcoming him with open arms, however, Jesus said a very strange thing. *'Foxes have holes and birds of the air have nests, but the Son of Man has nowhere to lay his head.'* What was that all about? Jesus sensed that something about the scribe's response was inadequate. This man's will was committed, and his affections were really set on the Lord, but Jesus realized that his **understanding** of what was involved in discipleship was inadequate. He did not really appreciate what the issues were, so Jesus spelled them out for him very, very clearly. 'If you follow Me, it means that, like Me, you will have no visible means of support. Now, how does it look?'

A wonderful thing about Jesus is that He always 'plays straight' with us. He does not call us on any hidden terms. He never tries to get us into a position where we could say 'If I had known it meant this, I would never have got involved in the first place.' Therefore, we can trust Him completely.

In the same passage in Matthew, there was another potential disciple standing by, and he said, *'Lord, first let me go and bury my father.'* To this man Jesus said, *'Follow me, and let the dead bury their own dead.'* What did He mean that time? This man's understanding of what was going to be involved in following Jesus was quite clear – he'd just heard about that. His will was ready to be committed too, but his **affections** were still tangled up. Part of him yearned for the Lord but part of him clung to his parents. So the Lord had to show him that he needed to sort out his emotional priorities.

Then in Mark chapter 10 we read of the rich young ruler who came running up to Jesus. In an outburst of eager affection, he fell on his knees and asked the Lord the way to eternal life. We are particularly told that Jesus felt love for this young man, and I am sure it was reciprocated. Little was wrong with his understanding of the law of God, but there was one thing lacking. Jesus touched it infallibly: *'Go, sell everything you have and give it to the poor, and you will have treasure in heaven. Then come, follow me.'* At the point of commitment the young man failed. He was not **willing**: *'At this the man's face fell. He went away sad, because he had great wealth.'*

In each case something was lacking from the total response required by Jesus.

	Understanding (mind)	*Affections (emotions)*	*Commitment (will)*
The scribe	✗	✓	✓
The other disciple	✓	✗	✓
The rich young ruler	✓	✓	✗

In the following pages we will explore further some of the implications of salvation for the whole person.

PART I

Chapter 1

The Mind of the Christian

Thank God that, as the Holy Spirit has been touching the church around the world, so many people have recovered the reality of spiritual experience. For generations the gospel was presented almost entirely as a set of intellectual and ethical propositions. Now we are realizing what has always been clear from Scripture: that knowledge of God comes primarily as revelation to the human spirit, not as information to the mind.

> 'No eye has seen,
>   no ear has heard,
> no mind has conceived
>   what God has prepared for those who love him.' –
> but God has revealed it to us by his Spirit.
>   The Spirit searches all things, even the deep things of God
> ... The man without the Spirit does not accept the things
> that come from the Spirit of God, for they are foolishness to
> him, and he cannot understand them, because they are
> spiritually discerned.   (1 Corinthians 2:9–10, 14)

This has far-reaching consequences for our whole Christian experience. We know that biblical faith is not a leap in the dark; it is not a determination to believe without evidence. On the contrary, it rests on solid evidence: it is a response to a revelation of God's will, 'seen' by our spirit in the way that Paul talks about it in 1 Corinthians 2. The great faith chapter in the New Testament, Hebrews 11, similarly underlines that 'seeing' is believing.

But this revelation-knowledge is neither reached by intellectual reasoning, nor, as Paul points out, is it regarded by the natural mind as trustworthy. Christians whose apprehension of the gospel is almost entirely intellectual, often find faith a great problem. I have a friend who describes such folk as 'intellectually handicapped Christians'. The intellect often gets in the way and handicaps faith.

Now, there is much truth in all this, but it is not the whole truth. We can fall into an equally dangerous error of thinking that all we need in order to walk with the Lord is a spirit – 'forget about the intellect', they say, 'it only creates problems'. 'Big mind, big problems; little mind, little problems; no mind, no problems!' seems to be the attitude. Anti-intellectualism of this kind can be truly disastrous.

The mind of human beings remains the strategic battleground in the universe. The struggle to dominate the mind is the struggle to dominate the entire human being. Christians today **must** understand clearly the function of the human mind, the problems it faces and – most important of all – the provision God has made for its redemption.

The function of the mind

The mind is the main communication center of the personality. What goes on in our mind substantially determines the kind of person we are. Proverbs 23:7 says, *'For as he thinks within himself, so he is.'* What we think determines what we do; what we do determines what we become.

> The Lord saw how great man's wickedness on the earth had become, and that every inclination of the thoughts of his heart was only evil all the time.   (Genesis 6:5)

Into the communication center of the mind there floods, from different sources, a whole mass of information inputs, impressions and messages. The mind is continuously analyzing, evaluating and passing judgement on these inputs. Many

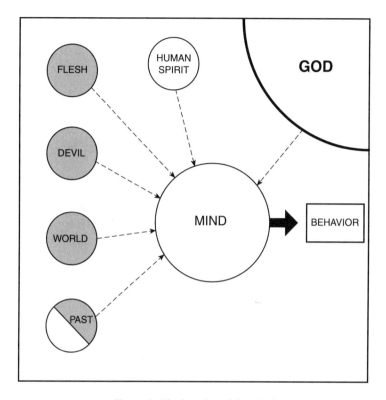

Figure 1: *The function of the mind*

– probably the vast majority – are screened out or disregarded; others are considered and rejected; some are filed away for future reference; but the selected ones are presented to the will for decision. Those that are accepted ultimately result in behavior of one kind or another. The diagram in Figure 1 illustrates this process.

Sources of our thought life

Figure 1 also draws attention to another very important aspect of our thought life. If we want to understand the problems we face in the mind, we have to trace the flood of thoughts and impressions back to their sources. In other words, where does the raw material of our thought life come from?

> [Jesus said], *'No good tree bears bad fruit, nor does a bad tree bear good fruit. Each tree is recognized by its own fruit.'*
> (Luke 6:43–44a)

Let us examine some of these sources in a little more detail.

The world

Information from the external environment is relayed to the mind through the senses. A lot of it is morally neutral, or non-moral: for example, the state of the weather, the color of a dress or the taste of food. Nevertheless, it may be interesting, frightening, delightful or humorous.

But there is also the world of which Jesus said that its *'deeds are evil'.* (John 3:19) This '**world**' comprises the whole condition of human affairs in rebellion against God and alienated from His life. It includes the culture, the economic system, the technology and the politics of human life. Daily we are exposed to its pressures and its influence, its value judgements, its opinions and its propaganda. Through radio, television, books, conversation, music, newspapers, billboards and the Internet, our minds are exposed to its outlook and its ways of looking at things. Let us have no illusions about the world's true character.

> *We know that we are children of God, and that **the whole world is under the control of the evil one**.*
> (1 John 5:19)

> *. . . This is the spirit of the antichrist, which you have heard is coming and even now **is already in the world**.*
> (1 John 4:3)

I am convinced that Christians do not sufficiently cultivate a critical attitude towards what they see and hear. The technique of the media is often so subtle and attractive that we can be taken in by it and never realize the content of what is being presented to us. Our minds can be bent without our being aware of what is happening.

The mind-set of the world is not something that we lose automatically when we become Christians. I remember a young man standing up in a meeting in the Netherlands and confessing, 'I have been a Christian for four years, but this week the Lord has shown me I have been thinking like a pagan all that time.'

The flesh

When used in its moral or spiritual sense, '**the flesh**' does not mean the human body. It is the world within, rather than the world without, the internal rather than the external environment. In the New Testament, *'flesh'*, or the *'sinful nature'*, as the NIV puts it, is the sum of all the desires, appetites, needs and drives that make for self-gratification. Through the fall it has become the principle of sin in human beings.

> *So I find this law at work: When I want to do good, evil is right there with me. For in my inner being I delight in God's law; but I see another law at work in the members of my body, waging war against the law of my mind and making me a prisoner of the law of sin at work within my members.*
> (Romans 7:21–23)

In the classic analysis of temptation in James chapter 1, the flesh figures prominently. Verses 14 and 15 state:

> *But each one is tempted when, by his own evil desire, he is dragged away and enticed. Then, after desire has conceived, it gives birth to sin; and sin, when it is full-grown, gives birth to death.*

The flesh is revealed as quite incorrigible in its enmity towards God.

> *The sinful nature is hostile to God. It does not submit to God's law, nor can it do so. Those controlled by the sinful nature cannot please God.* (Romans 8:7–8)

For the flesh to be gratified, it has first to capture the mind. Every sin, as Jesus pointed out in the Sermon on the Mount, is first of all a sin in the mind.

Satan

The devil has access to the mind of human beings. Whether we like it or not, it is part of the situation into which we have been born. Paul recognized clearly that the minds of Christians are also exposed to attack from this source.

> *But I am afraid that just as Eve was deceived by the serpent's cunning, **your minds** may somehow be led astray from your sincere and pure devotion to Christ.*
>
> (2 Corinthians 11:3)

The devil uses this access to plant temptations in our minds.

Sometimes Christians are terribly upset by the ghastly, horrible thoughts that come into their minds. They wonder, 'How can I be a child of God when I think such terrible things?' Yet many times such thoughts do not come from within us at all, evil though the flesh is. In fact, they come from the devil. We are not responsible for the thoughts, because they did not originate with us – but we are responsible if we harbor them, for that is within our power.

The Scriptures disclose a threefold satanic strategy in the onslaught on the mind:

1. **Suggestion** In Mark chapter 8 we are told how, when Jesus spoke plainly to the disciples regarding the cross, Peter took Him aside and began to rebuke Him. Jesus immediately recognized the source of Peter's thoughts on the matter, and said: *'Get behind me, Satan...'*. The devil's aim is that the thoughts planted in the mind will eventually result in sin. Thus, in Acts chapter 5, Ananias, deceiving the community regarding the price received for his property, has his sin put in its correct perspective by Peter: *'Ananias, how is it that Satan has so filled your heart that you have lied to the Holy Spirit...?'*

2. **Interference** The devil seeks to take out of our minds the word of God. In Mark 4:15 the seed that fell beside the road speaks of those in whom the word is sown: *'...as soon as they hear it, Satan comes and takes away the word that was sown in them.'*

3. **Domination** This is the devil's ultimate goal when the mind is taken captive and flooded with compulsive, obsessive thoughts. People with this problem are held in the *'... trap of the devil, who has taken them captive to do his will'* (2 Timothy 2:26).

The human spirit

The mind is also open to a stream of messages and impressions that come from our human spirit. It is important to understand that, although human beings are described in Ephesians as *'... dead in your transgressions and sins'*, the spirit of unregenerate people has not ceased to exist. Human beings still have a spirit. However, in the Bible, life and death are always a matter of relationship. Life means to be related through Christ to God, who is the source of uncreated life. Death means being cut off from God because of sin.

Thus, the human spirit, although in a state of death, still exists and still functions. It is still capable of contacting the realm of the spirit world. But because a person is in a state of death, he can reach only those spirit beings which are also in a state of death, that is, evil spirits. For this reason the Bible totally prohibits spiritualism and divination in all their forms, because people are so vulnerable to occult enslavement.

The main forms in which messages come from the human spirit to the mind are:

1. **The voice of conscience** Conscience is not the voice of God, nor is it infallible. It is the function of the human spirit that is able to apprehend general, moral truth and apply it to specific instances of our behavior. Conscience views what we are about to do, or what we have done, and says, 'That's wrong' or, 'That's right' (see Romans 2:15).

2. **Intuition** This is the immediate perception, judge-
    ment or insight that comes directly without any
    apparent intermediate mental steps. It may range all
    the way from indefinable promptings to flashes of
    sudden and creative insight. Remember that here we
    are not talking about the voice of the Holy Spirit, but
    purely about the way in which the natural human spirit
    functions. Some people are more intuitive than others.
    Many women are more intuitive than most men, which
    is why in many cases they are also more spiritual than
    men.

The voice of God

Human beings, for all our sin and rebellion, have never
managed to get out of the reach of God. That is our only
hope. Whenever God calls us to Himself, we are still within
the sound of God's voice. We communicate by reaching out
in our spirits to one another. The Holy Spirit is God reaching
out to us. *'The Spirit,'* Jesus said, *'...goes out from the Father'*
(John 15:26).

We may recognize His voice, sometimes by a painfully
awakened conscience responding to His judgment, sometimes by a direct intuitive impression. For the Christian, the
importance of knowing the voice of God and being able to
separate and distinguish this from the competing impressions in the mind is of extreme importance. *'The sheep,'* said
Jesus, *'listen to my voice. But they will never follow a stranger; in
fact, they will run away from him because they do not recognize a
stranger's voice'* (John 10:27 & 10:5). The way in which the
problem in the mind can be resolved so that the voice of God
can be heard, is the central theme of the renewed mind.

The past

In addition to all the sources mentioned, we have to allow for
the time dimension.

In other words, not only does the mind receive inputs from
the present, but it receives messages from the past, in the
form of memories. Some we try to recall, others come
unbidden and unwelcomed. Past failures still accuse us. Old

griefs still pain us. We are tantalized with long-lost joys or haunted by dreams and ambitions that have never yet materialized.

For some, the past is the most powerful attraction of all. This is because memory tends to be selective. It was the recollection of the 'good old days' in Egypt that was the most fertile breeding ground for discontent among the Israelites in the wilderness: they remembered the fish they used to eat free in Egypt, the cucumbers and the melons and the leeks and onions and the garlic (Numbers 11:5). What happened to the bondage – and the mud bricks and the murdered babies?

Memory is, of course, also a positive influence. The memory of past blessings can give life to present-day faith and obedience. In fact, the constant call of the prophets in the days of Israel's backsliding was 'Remember...' *'Remember how the Lord brought our fathers out of Egypt; remember how he led them into the Land of Promise.'* And, supremely, Jesus' words at the Last Supper *'Do this in remembrance of me'* (Luke 22:19), confirm the hallowing power of God-centered remembering.

When all this has been said, however, the real problem in the mind is neither the quantity of information it has to handle, nor its complexity. What that problem is, we now have to discover.

Chapter 2

The Blinded Mind

So far we have seen that the mind is faced with the task of receiving, sorting and passing on an endless stream of impressions, messages and communications. The mind does this not once but a thousand times a day. Even when we are asleep, not all levels of the mind shut down. There are sections of it that seem to work a continuous 24-hour shift.

The quantity and diversity of the message input is not, however, the real difficulty that the mind has to face. The real problem lies elsewhere. Without the revelation of the Bible, though, we would not realize that something has happened to the human mind. Let us see what the real problem is.

Romans 6:16 has the key to this mystery, yet it escaped me for many years.

> *Don't you know that when you offer yourselves to someone to obey him as slaves, you are slaves to the one whom you obey – whether you are slaves to sin, which leads to death, or to obedience, which leads to righteousness?*

The essential meaning of this principle can be expressed in a three-word phrase: **obedience creates authority**.

In other words, whatever we habitually obey becomes authoritative in our lives. It is, in fact, our obedience that establishes and confirms its authority over us.

I first learned this principle when helping to run a coffee-house in Wellington, New Zealand for Teen Challenge. It occupied an upstairs room in an old, wooden building in Cuba Street. My object lesson occurred one Friday evening just before 5 November (Guy Fawkes Day), a time when fireworks were readily available. That particular night the room was packed with kids from some of the motorcycle gangs. About nine o'clock somebody started tossing lighted firecrackers. That scared me, for I had visions of the old place going up in flames and the narrow stairway down to the street piled with bodies. Before I was really aware of what I was doing, I got up on the little stage, turned off the taped music and announced, 'Now, that's enough. Do a stupid thing like that again, and I shut this place down – and you're all out on the street!'

Then I had another look at the size of some of those kids against my own frame. One or two of the smaller ones I could have handled – but only one at a time! I went back to the kitchen praying desperately, 'Please Lord – no more crackers.'

I think the silence lasted just long enough for the 'cracker-merchant' to light the next firework with the butt of his cigarette. There were screams from the girls, roars of laughter and a lot of eager, expectant faces turned to see what I was going to do.

Now, I was on the spot because I had already stated my intentions. Trying to look a lot more confident that I felt, I walked back to the stage, switched the music off and said, 'That's it. We're closed for the night. Now, everybody, out!'

I more than half-expected them to wreck the place; but, to my astonishment, they got to their feet – all fifty or sixty of them – and, grumbling and complaining, trooped down the stairs and out into the cold city streets. I rushed down after them and locked the door in case they decided to come back!

I was climbing back up the stairs thanking the Lord for the exercise of His authority over those kids when He said, 'It wasn't My authority, it was yours.' He began to show me the working of this principle that has radically affected my life ever since. What had controlled those kids was in fact **the authority that they had given me**. I started to realize what Paul meant when he wrote those verses in Romans chapter 6.

This is what had happened. All the time I had been running the coffeehouse, there were certain things I would not let the kids do. For example, I wouldn't let them put their feet on the tables. (After all, they were small tables and their feet were usually large!) Nor would I let them hammer the keys of the piano, nor make out with their girlfriends. I found a lot of shy children hidden behind brazen exteriors. Because none of these things were of very great importance to them, and because I think they knew I really cared for them, they had got into the habit of doing what I said; and by these acts of obedience they had created in me, all unwittingly, a real authority. When it came to a showdown, the authority they had created was somehow too powerful for them to disobey.

They taught me a basic biblical principle: that authority is established by obedience. Whatever we habitually obey thereby possesses a binding authority over our minds. If we want the word of God to have authority in our life, there is only one way: obey it. If we want the Holy Spirit to have authority in our life, there is only one way: obey Him. If we always obey impulses of fear or doubt or resentment, what will have authority over our minds? Fear, doubt and resentment.

Who has seized authority?

Now can you begin to see the real nature of the problem in the human mind? It is not temptation alone. The real problem is that people, by our obedience to these temptations, have created in them and in their source a binding authority, so that they exercise rule and dominion over our minds.

Here are the authorities set up in the human mind:

The world

Through our obedience, the world has become more than an external source of temptation. Its values, its standards, and its ethos become internalized. Basic worldly assumptions cause us to believe that our happiness or wellbeing depends on what we can get for ourselves. God then has no place in our scheme of things. Our thinking becomes conformed to the world.

The flesh

In the same way, the flesh, or sinful nature, with its innate opposition to the ways of God, has been given authority over the mind. Self-seeking becomes the habitual base from which all decisions and judgements are made. The mind becomes, as Paul puts it in Romans 8:5, *'set on what the sinful nature desires'* and automatically at enmity against God.

The devil

Furthermore, in capitulating to the world system we have capitulated to Satan, who is ruler of the world. The flesh responds happily to the self-seeking philosophy of the world and likewise gives an opening for Satan to exploit. That is,

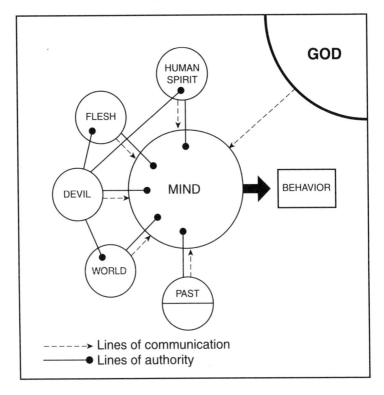

Figure 2: The unregenerate (blinded) mind

then, the fatal and fateful position of humanity, illustrated in Figure 2.

> *As for you, you were dead in your transgressions and sins, in which you used to live when you followed the ways of this world and of the ruler of the kingdom of the air, the spirit who is now at work in those who are disobedient. All of us also lived among them at one time, gratifying the cravings of our sinful nature and following its cravings and thoughts.*
> (Ephesians 2:1–3)

The devil has made deadly use of the authority that has been given him to shut up the human mind against God. The mind is blinded against truth. The Bible is quite clear that a person's first problem with the gospel is not being unwilling to believe but being unable to understand.

> *The god of this age has blinded the minds of unbelievers, so that they cannot see the light of the gospel of the glory of Christ, who is the image of God.* (2 Corinthians 4:4)

This is often evident when speaking to people about Christ. They hear the words, they understand the grammatical sense of what you are saying, but somehow the truth that the words convey cannot be comprehended. This is satanically devised blindness which human eloquence and persuasion is quite unable to penetrate.

People are thus in a hopeless position. They cannot find God because the satanic dominion in their minds is set to keep them blinded against divine truth. They cannot break free from this mental bondage even if they want to, because they are under an authority that will not let them go. Paradoxically, the struggle to get rid of hateful thoughts can even generate guilt feelings, because it is seen as rebellion against legitimate authority.

Repentance: the change of mind

With all this in view, it is significant that the root meaning of the New Testament word for repentance, *metanoia*, is 'a change of mind'. Praise God! The devil's hold on the human mind is powerless against the Light of the world. *'The light shines in the darkness, and the darkness has not overcome it'* (John 1:5).

In spite of all that Satan can do, the Holy Spirit is able to penetrate the darkened mind and call people to repentance. So helpless are we in ourselves, that even repentance is described as a gift of God. The conclusion drawn by the apostles and brethren in Jerusalem, after hearing Peter's account of the outpouring of the Spirit on the household of Cornelius, was, *'So then, God has granted even the Gentiles repentance unto life'* (Acts 11:18).

In writing to Timothy, Paul has the same understanding of the human situation. He counsels Timothy to correct with gentleness those who are in opposition:

> *. . . in the hope that God will grant them repentance leading them to a knowledge of the truth, and that they will come to their senses and escape from the trap of the devil, who has taken them captive to do his will.*
>
> (2 Timothy 2:25–26)

When people repent and commit themselves in an act of personal trust to Christ, they are born from above by the power of the Holy Spirit. Their hearts and minds are illuminated by the light of God's presence.

> *For God, who said, 'Let light shine out of darkness', made his light shine in our hearts to give us the light of the knowledge of the glory of God in the face of Christ.*
>
> (2 Corinthians 4:6)

In the recreated spirit of the believer, the Holy Spirit now dwells. As He illuminates the human spirit, the conscience now begins to deal with the mind. It becomes sensitive to sin and disobedience. Repentance and confession lead to forgiveness and cleansing. As He is obeyed, the Holy Spirit gains authority in the mind, opening it to understand the Scriptures. The mind is now enlightened.

The enlightened but double mind

Often a very strong experience of grace at conversion has a powerful effect in ridding the mind of the domination and authoritative power of sinful habits. But this is not always the case. Like Lazarus after he came out of the grave, we often remain bound by the grave-clothes.

Furthermore, the world, the flesh and the devil are constantly striving to regain ground that has been lost. Thus it is the painful experience of most Christians to find – long after conversion perhaps – that many old bondages either persist in the mind, or (through failure to walk in victory) are re-established by the same principle of obedience.

The state of mind that results is illustrated in Figure 3. Some areas are full of light and open to the Lord, while others

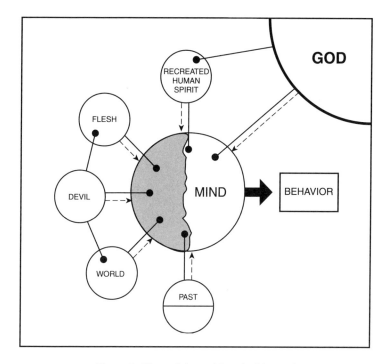

Figure 3: The enlightened but double mind

are dominated by darkness. Between the two, the dividing line is a kind of moving frontier which reflects the vitality or otherwise of our experience of the moment. There is war in the mind.

In this condition, although the mind is open to the revelation of divine truth and the prompting of the Holy Spirit, it is open to other things as well. Old thought patterns or temptations surprise us by their persistence, and wear us down into a state of defeat and despair.

Areas of the mind, we discover, are still under the control of the old masters. Into these areas they inject their poison. The flesh wars against the spirit and the spirit against the flesh. The battleground is the mind. Whoever captures that wins the battle for or against temptation.

Chapter 3

The Renewed Mind

The mind we have been describing was essentially what I was personally struggling with for years. There were times of growth and blessing when light surged in and the darkness retreated. There were spiritual 'lows' when the light was almost swamped by the resurgence of old problems. The frontier was exactly that described in James 1, like the surf of the sea, continually advancing and retreating.

> ... he who doubts is like a wave of the sea, blown and tossed by the wind ... he is a double-minded man, unstable in all he does.
> (James 1:6, 8)

He was right. A mind like this, I discovered, has a built-in instability. How, for example, could I tell whether a particular impression in my mind came from:

- the Holy Spirit, or
- my own fleshly desires seeking fulfillment, or
- Satan (perhaps as an angel of light) trying to deceive me?

'If it is from God, it will bring peace,' I would be told. That was really little help. In my mind, peace was a very relative and variable thing. So was the difference between light and dark, or order and confusion.

I would read a verse like Philippians 2:5, *'Your attitude should be the same as that of Christ Jesus...'* and wonder how on earth I could achieve that. Worse still was 1 Corinthians 2:16: *'But we have the mind of Christ.'* I could see no way in which the mental turmoil and uncertainty within my mind could, by any stretch of imagination, be the mind of Jesus in me.

It was in this condition that one day I came across two very familiar passages of Scripture. I had read them many times before but somehow had never realized their real significance. The first was Romans 12:2:

> *Do not conform any longer to the pattern of this world, but be transformed by the renewing of your mind Then you will be able to test and approve what God's will is – his good, pleasing, and perfect will.*

Here I saw that in some way Paul linked both freedom from conformity to the world system, and the certainty about knowing the will of God, with the mind being renewed.

Had my mind been renewed? I knew it hadn't. Was I able to prove what the will of God was for my life? No, I couldn't. The second passage was from Ephesians 4:22–24:

> *... put off your old self, which is being corrupted by its deceitful desires ... be made new in the attitude of your minds; and ... put on the new self, created to be like God in true righteousness and holiness.*

For the very first time I saw that there were three stages here, not two:

- Stage 1 – lay aside the old self.
- Stage 2 – be renewed in the spirit of your mind.
- Stage 3 – put on the new self.

I began to see that all along I had been trying to jump from Stage 1 to Stage 3 in one leap, bypassing Stage 2. In so doing, I had left an enemy in the rear with power to cut the lines of communication and bring my spiritual advance to a grinding halt any time he chose.

At the same time, the idea of renewal for the tangle of my mind seemed almost too good to be true. Was it really possible for God to undo and sweep away deeply ingrained patterns of thinking, and change my mental habits? After all, the mind continually patterns the very information we receive according to those very habits.

Let me show you what I mean. Take an ordinary kitchen saucer and set it full of gelatin. Now pour a spoonful of hot liquid over the gelatin. Notice that as the liquid runs over the jelly, it melts a pattern of little grooves or channels. If you then pour a second spoonful of liquid over the gelatin, this liquid will not run just anywhere. It will flow down the channels that are already there.

Now, the mind will channel information that it receives in a similar way. What we receive conforms to the already existing configurations in our minds. A hundred people hearing the same words will receive them in a hundred different ways. The same thing can amuse one person, offend another, please a third and irritate a fourth. Their various responses depend entirely on the way in which their minds pattern the information. Could anything, I wondered really eradicate these deeply etched thought patterns?

For example, I had one particularly embarrassing mental characteristic: a life-long habit of daydreaming. As a small boy I was shy and rather timid. I always seemed to be in classes among boys two or three years older, which made things worse. I also had a fertile imagination so that, as often happens, I made for myself a safe mental world where I wasn't afraid of anything because I had made it all.

As I grew up, I grew out of most of my timidity and shyness but I was left with an incurable tendency to daydream. From time to time this got me into quite some bother. There seemed nothing much that I could do about it, however, and eventually resigned myself to the fact that that was just the way I was. I would be a daydreamer till the day I died, it seemed.

Today I no longer daydream. If I try to, it is as though my mind says, 'Where are you trying to push me? I don't know the way anymore.' In many more serious matters than daydreaming, I have found that we need not be stuck with our old thought patterns, no matter how deeply ingrained they have become. I have discovered from the Bible (and tested it in my own experience) that our minds can be renewed so that they are freed up to think according to the mind of Christ. In fact, it is more than an offer – it is a command twice repeated, *'Be transformed by the renewing of your mind...'* (Romans 12:2); *'Be made new in the attitude of your mind...'* (Ephesians 4:23). Therefore, we cannot doubt but that it is meant for us to experience.

Let me show you how this can be your experience, too.

God's provision for human need

God's provision to meet every need of the human race is always found in two divine works or actions:

1.   The work of the cross
2.   The work of the Spirit

Both are essential and they go together. Without the work of the cross, there is no way in which the life and love of God can reach and save ruined humanity. There is no basis on which the Holy Spirit can deal with us.

> *'For the message of the cross is foolishness to those who are perishing, but to those who are being saved it is the power of God.'*   (1 Corinthians 1:18)

This cannot be overemphasized. Any psychological understanding or means of obtaining wholeness or healing that bypasses the work of Calvary is doomed to failure. The same is true of any type of 'deeper life' teaching that holds out the prospect of sanctification without the work of the cross being central. It will lead to ultimate frustration.

But, without the work of the Holy Spirit, the great, objective, finished work of Calvary would remain experientially ineffective. It is the Holy Spirit who takes the things of Christ and reveals them to us. It is He who from within us makes real in experience what Jesus died to secure for us.

The work of the cross

Human sin made the cross a necessity. We understand that much. What we often do not understand, however, is the magnitude of what Jesus did on the cross. He met **all** human needs. The fact that our sins have been forgiven is wonderful. We Christians can experience what it is to have a clean conscience in a guilt-ridden world. That is a marvelous thing. But the cross dealt with much more than the problem of our **sins** – it also dealt with the problem with our **sinfulness**.

In His humanity the Son of God was tempted in all points as we are, and for the 33 years of His life He won complete and total personal victory over sin and Satan. At the end He was able to say, '... *the prince of this world is coming. He has no hold on me'* (John 14:30).

In the man Jesus there was nothing that could give Satan any claim or any authority over Him: no sin, no failure, no yielding; yet this freedom and this victory were locked up in the individual humanity of Jesus.

But when Jesus came to the cross, His individual humanity became a corporate one – it incorporated all who would believe in Him. In John 12:32 Jesus said:

> *'But I, when I am lifted up from the earth, will draw all men to myself.'* He said this to show the kind of death he was going to die.

This is so crucial that it needs to be spelled out very explicitly in order that it is clearly understood. It is the key to our real freedom from the authority of our sins.

- Because we were incorporated into Christ, when He died, we died; when He bore the judgment of God on sin, our sins were judged; when He was buried, we were buried; when He rose, we rose; when He was exalted to the place of authority, we were placed there, too (Romans 6:3–6; Ephesians 2:5–6).

- On the cross Jesus yielded Himself to the power of darkness (Luke 22:53), but by His death and resurrection

He shattered that power forever over all the lives identified with Him.

In other words, the cross renders ineffective all the enslaving authorities that have taken charge of our minds. The Scriptures make this abundantly clear.

1. The world

For those who are in Christ, the cross nullifies the authority and domination of the world system. The principalities and powers that rule the world were defeated at Calvary.

> *And having disarmed the powers and authorities, he made a public spectacle of them, triumphing over them by the cross.*
> (Colossians 2:15)

> *May I never boast except in the cross of our Lord Jesus Christ, through which the world has been crucified to me, and I to the world.*   (Galatians 6:14)

I no longer have to submit to the authority of the world's values or fears or pressures. The cross cuts me off from them and cuts them off from me.

2. The flesh

Death frees us entirely from our slavery to the flesh. In Christ we experience that death which is liberating.

> *Those who belong to Christ Jesus have crucified the sinful nature with its passions and desires.*   (Galatians 5:24)

> *For we know that our old self was crucified with him so that the body of sin might be done away with, that we should no longer be slaves to sin – because anyone who has died has been freed from sin.*   (Romans 6:6–7)

It is not that the flesh as such has ceased to exist but that its authority over us ended at the cross. Incorporated into Christ, we died there with Him. And there the claim of the flesh on our obedience ended also. The resurrection life owes nothing to the flesh.

> *For we know that since Christ was raised from the dead, he*
> *cannot die again; death no longer has mastery over him. The*
> *death he died, he died to sin once for all...*
>
> (Romans 6:9–10)
>
> *The sting of death is sin...* (1 Corinthians 15:56)

3. The devil

The cross was Satan's downfall; his defeat there was total. The victory of Calvary applies to all those who were there, that is all those who were in Christ and died and rose in Him.

> *Since the children have flesh and blood, he too shared in*
> *their humanity so that by his death he might destroy him*
> *who holds the power of death – that is, the devil – and free*
> *those who all their lives were held in slavery by their fear of*
> *death.* (Hebrews 2:14–15)

The cross may have appeared to be the world's judgment on Christ. In fact, it was God's judgment on the world. Instead of being the devil's triumph, it was his eviction. In the light of His coming sacrifice Jesus could declare:

> *Now is the time for judgement on this world; now the prince of*
> *this world will be driven out. But I, when I am lifted up from*
> *the earth, will draw all men to myself.* (John 12:31–32)

4. The past

It needs to be clearly grasped that the cross stands between us and all our past. It does not blot the past out of our memory, but entirely robs it of its power over us.

> *For Christ's love compels us, because we are convinced that*
> *one died for all, and therefore all died ... Therefore, if*
> *anyone is in Christ, he is a new creation; the old has gone,*
> *the new has come!* (2 Corinthians 5:14, 17)

Sometimes we think our past, because it is beyond our reach to amend or alter, is also beyond God's power. That is not so. There are, in fact, three things that God wants to do with the negative things in our past. I do not know which of the three is the most wonderful but here they are:

- **First**, He wants to forgive us for our past. Calvary means full, free, total forgiveness. It means a cleansed conscience that no longer condemns us. Only the blood of Jesus is able to liberate us from the corrosive, crippling effects of conscious and unconscious guilt feelings.

- **Secondly**, God wants to free us from the power of the past so that we are not walking in the daily dread of past sins and past fears and past enemies spoiling our present experience. And that release is meant to be as total and as final as forgiveness.

- **Thirdly**, He wants to redeem our past. What do I mean by that? I mean that when we release our past into the wonderful hands of God somehow He will redeem everything that can be redeemed. I have seen Him bring good out of my mistakes and blunders. I have seen Him even bring good out of my sins. They still remain wrong but somehow He can make them profitable for His purposes. It does not excuse my sin but, oh, how it magnifies His grace!

Breaking free in our mind

For the work that Jesus did for us on the cross to become effective in our individual experience, it has to be personally appropriated. All believers have done this first when they accepted Christ as Savior, and accepted His death as securing forgiveness for our sins.

But the cross not only deals with forgiveness: it deals also with deliverance. And this, too, must be personally appropriated. It is the only way in which we can be set free from the domination of the authorities that rule in our minds. How do we do it?

The first step is to confess the sins of our mind and receive God's forgiveness. As you will see, we need to go further than forgiveness; but we must do this first. It means an honest confession of our wrong thoughts – whether anger, fear, lust, anxiety or remorse – and the acceptance of the blood-bought forgiveness of Calvary.

The second step is to renounce and reject the authority that, in our mind, we have given to the world, the flesh, the past or the devil. Note that **we** have to do it. We are not to ask God to do it for us. **We have to do it ourselves**. Read the following verse very carefully.

> *The weapons we fight with are not the weapons of the world. On the contrary, they have divine power to demolish strongholds. We demolish arguments and every pretension that sets itself up against the knowledge of God, and we take captive every thought to make it obedient to Christ.*
>
> (2 Corinthians 10:4, 5)

Make no mistake, if Christ had not rendered powerless all these alien authorities, there is no way we could ever come out from under their power. But, if we ourselves do not reject and renounce them, we remain under their power in spite of what the cross accomplished. We are the ones who must dismantle them because we are the ones who set them up in the first place. They will trade on that authority and hold us captive until we act upon our freedom in Christ.

I remember speaking once to a friend about the deliverance that there is for the believer from the power of sin. He said to me later, 'I went home that night and realized that I had been living in a prison for nearly twenty years – and the doors had been open all the time. Right there and then I walked out, a free man.'

Make the act of renunciation very specific and very definite. It is no place for general confessions or general prayers. You are dealing with individual authorities and specific problems. Confess it aloud until you really know in your heart that it is done.

'Satan I renounce you and all your works. In the name of Jesus I reject the hold of fear you have on my mind, because your authority was rendered powerless at Calvary. I take back right now every inch of ground I have yielded in my mind to fear and I bring all my thoughts under the lordship of Jesus Christ.'

Sometimes specific problems have to be dealt with. For instance, you may have to cast off a long-cherished grudge. That old hurt which you may have nursed for years will have to be relinquished. Some bitter incident from the past could be having a present grip on your mind. It will require attention. By continued bitterness against another you give that person domination over your mind and personality.

A woman confessed to me once that she had allowed the complaining and fractiousness of an elderly parent she was nursing to have such power over her mind, that she could not rid herself of resentful and unloving reactions. Only when that authority in her mind was broken could she come free, so that none of the querulousness of the parent could any longer disturb her peace of mind.

There are two specific instances in which we may need special ministry. I shall call the two cases 'bondage' and 'a curse'.

1. Bondage

None of us arrives on earth straight from the hand of God. In other words, we are each the product of past generations and from them we inherit, by nature or by nurture, certain character traits or behavioral tendencies. We may have a tendency towards moodiness or timidity or quick temper. We can usually recognize attitudes and traits in ourselves that were in our parents. We can see the same tendencies in our own children.

By no means are all of these characteristics bad. We inherit strengths as well as weaknesses. But if we have inherited a weakness in a certain area, and we ourselves yield along the line of that weakness, it creates a bondage that is far harder to break than any ordinary habit. The iniquity (not the guilt) of the fathers is visited on the children to the third and fourth generation.

In a number of counseling situations over the years I have often found this type of bondage to be a major factor in problems in the mind involving sexual fantasies, anger, depression, worry, bitterness and resentfulness. Occult involvement in particular often produces severe psychic disturbances and apparitions in the children and grandchildren. In most cases of bondage the person is struggling to lop off the leaves of the sin or temptation, but the taproot going back into the past fuels the problem. Because of this, repentance, prayer and resolution seem to have little effect.

Nevertheless the power of the past – even the pre-natal past – can be broken. In the name of Jesus the taproot can be cut and we can be loosed from the evil inheritance that seems to hold the source of the problem beyond our reach.

The important steps are these:

- Firstly we must accept responsibility for our sin in the particular area of failure. In spite of the inheritance, it is our own failure that has caused the problem and for this we need to repent and ask forgiveness without making any excuses.

- Secondly we must renounce the authority that we have allowed to become established in our mind. To this point the approach is the same as for all other problems in the mind.

- Thirdly we need to be prayed for, so that the link with our past inheritance is cut in the name of Jesus.

> *Therefore, if anyone is in Christ, he is a new creation; the old has gone, the new has come!* (2 Corinthians 5:17)

> *I will give you the keys of the kingdom of heaven; whatever you bind on earth will be bound in heaven, and whatever you loose on earth will be loosed in heaven.*
> (Matthew 16:19)

Our natural inheritance, with whatever weaknesses and sin there is in it, can be cut. We have, in fact, a new inheritance into which we can be planted. Our life now springs from a new source. Because we are born of God, the nature that we have inherited is the character of Jesus. That is the image to which we can now conform.

I have seen many people come into an experience of glorious freedom when the power of the past has been cut off in this way. For the first time they experience practicable, sustainable victory in areas of their life where before was total defeat. It does not remove temptation, but it certainly reduces it to the ordinary, manageable level that they can learn to struggle and overcome.

The final step eluded me for many years. Then one night in a house church communion service God quite suddenly spoke through a word of prophecy. He simply said, '**Honor your mother and your father**'. So we did just that. One by one each person honored his or her parents. Some had had good parents, some poor parents, in one or two cases people did not know their natural parents. But they honored their mother and father as the ones who gave them life and brought them to birth. In this role, even the worst parents represent to some degree the Father.

At the end God gave us another word. He said, 'What you have done tonight has reversed the curse.' What does this mean? The inheritance of sin and weakness handed down from generation to generation is a curse. But when we are freed from that and in our turn we give blessing and honor to those who have gone before, the bondage ends right there. Our children, present and future, are freed from the same bondage being handed down to them from us. In many cases since then this final act of obedience to the commandment has confirmed and established the person in a totally new God-given freedom from inherited chains.

2. Curses

There is another similar area in which specific ministry is often needed for a person to be set free. Words said to a person, often in their childhood and often by someone close to them (parent, family member or teacher, for example), have cut so deeply as to become a real curse or bane on their lives. *'Death and life'* says the Book of Proverbs *'is in the power of the tongue'*. I remember an elderly Anglican priest ministering with me one night on an altar call and saying to me afterwards, 'Tom, pray for me. There are things said to me as a boy in prep school in England that have stuck like hooks in my mind ever since.'

The binding, blighting power of such words is that they always have a certain measure of truth of them. Proverbs 26:2 says:

Like a fluttering sparrow or a darting swallow,
an undeserved curse does not come to rest.

The words of curses echo our own self-doubts – and that is what shackles them to us. And when those self-doubts are vocalized by someone we love or respect, they alight on our unsuspecting spirit with deadly effect. Cruel sarcasm, angry abuse, cutting jibes and even careless, thoughtless humor at another's expense can become a self-fulfilling prophecy years later.

But curses can be broken.

Christ redeemed us from the curse of the law by becoming a curse for us. (Galatians 3:13)

All these cruel, cursing words come from law in one or other of its forms. But, to redeem **us** Christ became a curse. Think for a moment of all the cutting, cruel things that were said about Jesus. They said He was a sinner, that He was illegitimate in His birth, that He was demon-possessed. In the letter to the Galatians, Paul quotes from Deuteronomy 21:23, which states that *'anyone who is hung on a tree is under God's curse.'* Jesus bore all human curses on humanity, as well as the curse of the law, and at the cross broke their hold on us. We can be loosed from the power of such words, through the power of the cross of Jesus.

Receiving the gift of a renewed mind

In the renewal of the mind it is the cross that breaks the power of the authorities that once ruled there; it is the Holy Spirit who renews our liberated mind.

We need to understand that the renewed mind is a gift. In the words of Paul (in the King James Version):

> *God has not given us the spirit of fear but of power and of love and of a sound mind.*   (2 Timothy 1:7)

We need also to realize that this renewal comes only by the working of the Holy Spirit.

> *He saved us, not because of righteous things we had done, but because of his mercy ... through the washing of rebirth and renewal by the Holy Spirit.*   (Titus 3:5)

In 2 Corinthians 3 Paul speaks of those who, like the Jews of his day, have a mind that is veiled when reading the Scripture. Then he says in verses 16 and 17:

> *'But whenever anyone turns to the Lord, the veil is taken away. Now the Lord is the Spirit, and where the Spirit of the Lord is, there is freedom.'*

As we consciously and deliberately yield up our mind to the presence of the Holy Spirit, He will wash out the old habitual thought patterns, the compulsive thoughts that claimed autonomy, and the weary treadmill of negativity. The bondage is broken, curses are lifted, and the mind is free. It becomes the renewed mind illustrated in Figure 4. It is a mind in which there is now only one authority, because its thoughts have been brought captive to the obedience of Christ. Paul describes it in Romans 8:6 as a mind that is *'set on what the Spirit desires'*.

Because the internal problem of authority has been resolved, the result is life and peace, and the peace of God becomes the guardian and the arbitrator.

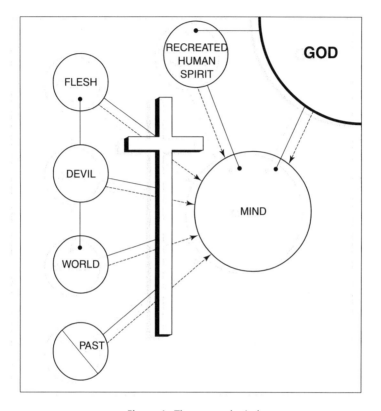

***Figure 4**: The renewed mind*

And the peace of God, which transcends all understanding, will guard your hearts and your minds in Christ Jesus.
(Philippians 4:7)

Let the peace of Christ rule in your hearts, since as members of one body you were called to peace. And be thankful.
(Colossians 3:15)

When an alien thought intrudes, its true source is readily identifiable, no matter how plausible it seems. Peace is disturbed. If you can deal with the intruder, however, then peace reigns again.

Once in a meeting, I had invited a Christian brother to minister, and the blessing of God was clearly on what he was saying. Then he skirted around a topic on which he knew we disagreed. The thought came into my mind, 'He's let me down. He's going to take advantage of the opportunity I've given him.'

In fact, he did not, but somehow there was a heavy feeling in my heart. I lifted it to the Lord and realized clearly what had happened. I had listened to a satanic slander against my brother – and I had harbored the thought. I confessed my sin, dispelled the thought, and instantly the joy and peace returned. Yet, the thought had been initially presented to my mind in the guise of pastoral prudence and concern.

The renewed mind becomes increasingly able to deal intelligently with the intuitions of the spirit, so that we can prove what the will of God is. If we try to deal with the intuitions of the spirit with an unrenewed mind, we are in grave danger of mistaking the product of our own mind with the intuitive perceptions of the voice of the Holy Spirit.

Retaining a renewed mind

It is important to realize that the renewal of the mind is not a once-for-all happening. It is a work of God that must be established in a continuous process. There are several import- ant points that we must understand.

The first is that when your mind is renewed, from there on **you decide what is going to occupy your mind.** Some people have become so accustomed to a mind that claims autonomy, that it comes as something of a surprise to find that we (and not our minds) are to determine what our minds think about. In Philippians 4:8, Paul says:

> ... *whatever is true, whatever is noble, whatever is right, whatever is pure, whatever is lovely, whatever is admirable – if anything is excellent or praiseworthy – think about such things.*

The mind is never meant to be passive. Peter counsels us, *'prepare your minds for action'* (1 Peter 1:13).

I spoke to a young Christian once who had come into all sorts of spiritual difficulty because when he first became a Christian someone had told him that, to hear the Lord speaking, all you had to do was to let your mind go a complete blank. Not surprisingly, all sorts of alarming and nonsensical things came flooding into the vacuum. The Christian mind should be active and eager. We should *'stimulate it to wholesome thinking'* (2 Peter 3:1), not let it go to sleep.

The second thing to realize is that the renewal of the mind **does not exempt us from temptation**. Look back at the diagram in Figure 4. The cross breaks the line of authority; it does **not** break the line of communication. Temptation will still come. The devil will try to have us believe that the old authorities still apply. Don't be fooled: the broken yoke is useless. But on the other hand, remember that because obedience creates authority, we can still be trapped into self-created bondage. If we realize that we are succumbing to wrong thoughts and setting up alien authorities, we can be released simply and effectively. We can and must retain our freedom.

Temptation of itself is not the real problem. The real problem is the place of authority that the temptation has in our minds. This is what makes the task of ejecting unwanted thoughts so difficult. Once we settle the question of authority, victory becomes an exciting reality.

Finally, we discover that renewing the mind is **not only a crisis but also a process**. This is a necessity of our human nature. We need not only to be made free, but to learn how to use freedom.

> *You, my brothers, were called to be free. But do not use your freedom to indulge the sinful nature; rather, serve one another in love.* (Galatians 5:13)

Once we have said the irrevocable 'yes' to the lordship of Christ in our minds, the renewing work of the Holy Spirit becomes a continuous experience.

> *. . . Put on the new self, which is being renewed in knowledge*
> *in the image of its Creator.*   (Colossians 3:10)

Out of this continuous renewing will come a continuous transformation. Paul sets it out in Romans 12:2. He expands his description of that transformation, in 2 Corinthians 3:18.

> *And we, who with unveiled faces all reflect the Lord's glory,*
> *are being transformed into his likeness with ever-increasing*
> *glory, which comes from the Lord, who is the Spirit.*

A mirror can reflect only what it beholds. Even so, we can only reflect in our lives as much of Christ as we 'see'. What we behold of Christ is determined by what we receive through the revelation of the Holy Spirit.

With our minds renewed and cleansed of all alien domination, we can then be conformed, not to the mold of the world system, but to God's mold: the likeness of His Son which is the glorified humanity of our Lord Jesus Christ.

PART II

Chapter 4

What About Our Feelings?

There is probably no area of our personality where we need more help – and receive less – than in the area of the emotions or feelings. Generally, Christian teaching has taken a fairly negative attitude towards the whole subject. We may, in some churches, allow freedom of expression for joy and praise in worship, but this is still regarded by others as rank 'emotionalism'. Even where expression in worship is encouraged, there remains a very tentative and uncertain outlook towards the emotions as a whole.

The title of a book, *Our Rebel Emotions*, probably sums up the general view. We tend to keep our feelings on a tight leash because we are not very sure what would happen if we let them loose. At the same time we are subconsciously aware of the constriction that this produces within us. We get 'hung up' or 'uptight' about things.

I remember speaking at a house meeting in a Christian community working among young people in one city. There was a free and beautiful expression of praise and worship in the meeting, and those present were being encouraged to open themselves in this way to the Lord. But afterwards, when talking to the head of the community about their work, I heard him say, 'There is one thing we are very strong on here – no feelings.'

I think I know what he was trying to say, but his remark illustrates our very ambivalent attitude towards this powerful and important part of our nature. Books for young Christians stress repeatedly that the Christian life is one of faith, not feelings; although the contrast Paul makes in 2 Corinthians 5:7 is between faith and sight, not faith and feelings. *'We live by faith, not by sight.'*

Of course, we are not meant to take feelings as the sole (or even the main) guide to truth and reality; but neither are we meant to ignore them. The difficulty is that we cannot be selective. If we ignore, repress or suppress the emotional side of our nature, we damage positive feelings as well as negative ones. That is why many Christians do not **feel** that God loves them or that they love God, although they **know** that at least the former is true.

What are the emotions?

The emotions are more easily experienced than described. Perhaps the simplest way of understanding them is to see them as the total response of the person to happenings in our environment. Thus a sudden noise makes you afraid, an insult makes you angry or the sight of a person in pain causes you to feel pity.

For example, suppose I am wandering peacefully across a field, when suddenly, out of the corner of my eye, I see a large, black animal with a leg on each corner and a pair of handlebars out front! This animal has clearly mistaken me for a red rag and is hastening to do something drastic about it. Do I sit down and make a series of rational calculations as to the bull's course, speed and weight, and the probable consequences of impact? No! What happens is that under the powerful stimulus of an emotional state – raw fear – I depart for the nearest fence at a speed that might qualify me for the Olympic Games!

Not all emotions mobilize the body's entire resources to cope with an emergency as do fear, or anger, but they all have this factor of total response to stimuli. The response that we experience in such situations is accompanied by an affect: that is, a feeling of some kind. Depending on the strength of the feeling, there may also be physical sensations or changes. If we are angry, we may get red in the face and find our muscles growing tense. If we are nervous our mouth may get dry and our palms begin to perspire.

Isaiah has a very vivid description of some physiological results of extreme emotional stress.

> *At this my body is racked with pain,*
> *pangs seize me, like those of a woman in labor;*
> *I am staggered by what I hear,*
> *I am bewildered by what I see.*
> *My heart falters,*
> *fear makes me tremble...*   (Isaiah 21:3–4)

Another important aspect of the emotions is that, once activated by a set of circumstances, the same feelings can be repeated time and time again merely by recalling the event. A situation that caused us fear or shame can still bring anxiety or embarrassment every time we remember it even years later. It is this repetitive effect, particularly with the strong negative emotions that produce physiological changes, which can be the source of a whole range of functional and organic disorders.

The emotions and behavior

Emotions are very powerful motivators of behavior, as Scripture clearly indicates:

> *Above all else, guard your heart,*
> *for it is the wellspring of life.*   (Proverbs 4:23)

In spite of the cherished idea most of us have that we make decisions on the basis of logical reasoning, every salesman and every advertiser knows that to bring people to the point of decision-making you have to move their feelings. Generally the rational faculties are used afterwards to find reasons to justify the decisions we wanted to make.

In analyzing the emotions, it is useful to classify them according to:

1.   whether they are pleasant or unpleasant, and
2.   whether they attract us towards or repel us from the thing that caused them.

You can plot the whole range of human emotions on the scales shown in Figure 5.

Peace, for example, is a pleasant emotion. It attracts us to the person or experience that produces it. Anger is an unpleasant emotion that repels us from whatever arouses it. Joy is a very pleasant, very attractive emotion. Fear is unpleasant and generally repels, although sometimes we are morbidly attracted to the very thing that scares us. That is why there is always a market for horror films or murder mysteries. In fact,

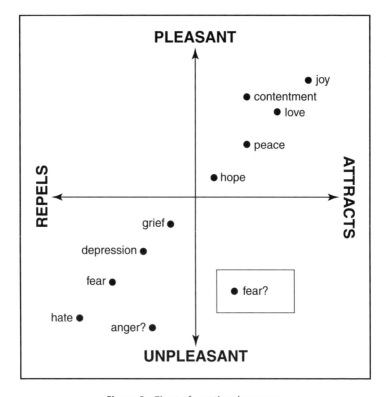

Figure 5: *Chart of emotional responses*

other negative emotions such as sadness and anger can be strangely attractive to us if they are familiar, and fill the place of more taboo emotions.

Naturally we prefer pleasant emotions to unpleasant ones. We respond more positively to things that attract us than to things that repel us. But we have to learn a very important lesson. When we apply moral or ethical values to emotional states, we can get into serious difficulties. If we regard all pleasant emotions as 'good', and all unpleasant emotions as 'bad', confusion follows. A person caught up in a morally wrong or sinful relationship will sometimes say, 'How can this possibly be wrong when it makes me feel so good?'

Get this clear. An emotion is not morally good because it is pleasant. Nor, on the other hand, is it good because it is unpleasant.

All emotions, whether they be pleasant or unpleasant, whether they attract or repel, may be either good or bad, right or wrong. This is so important that we need to have it substantiated from the Scriptures.

Love, we might think, must surely always be good.

> *Dear friends, let us love one another, for love comes from God.*
> *Everyone who loves has been born of God and knows God.*
> (1 John 4:7)

Yet there is a completely wrong kind of love. In the same epistle it says:

> *Do not love the world or anything in the world. If anyone*
> *loves the world, the love of the Father is not in him.*
> (1 John 2:15)

And, in case we are in doubt as to what is meant by love, John uses *'agapao'*, *agapé* love, in both verses. Yes, there can be a wrong kind of *agapé* love.

Anger is an unpleasant emotion towards which we generally make a negative moral judgment.

> *You have heard that it was said to the people long ago, 'Do*
> *not murder, and anyone who murders will be subject to*

*judgment.' But I tell you that anyone who is angry with his
brother will be subject to judgment.*   (Matthew 5:21–22)

A friend of mine, speaking on this passage, told how he
was preparing a sermon one wet Saturday afternoon, badly
distracted by the noise his two small children were making.
Finally irritation got the better of him and he heard himself
shouting at his two boys 'If you don't stop that racket, I'll kill
you!' Later he commented, 'Out of my own lips God showed
me how close anger is to murder'.

And yet Ephesians 4:26 says, *'In your anger do not sin'*. In
other words, we can be angry without sinning. In the
synagogue where there was a man with a withered hand,
Jesus looked round at the Pharisees *'in anger and deeply
distressed at their stubborn hearts'* (Mark 3:5). If we can see
cruelty to human beings or animals without being angry,
there is something wrong with our moral sensibilities. Anger,
in other words, can be good or bad.

Peace, surely, is always good. Did not Jesus say, *'Peace I
leave with you, my peace I give you'* (John 14:27)? We often tell
people that if they have peace about something, God must
surely be in it. But there is another peace the Bible talks about
– the quiet of hopeless bondage, or the complacency of false
peace:

> *'They dress the wound of my people as though it were not
>   serious.
> "Peace, peace," they say, when there is no peace.'*
> (Jeremiah 6:14)

Fear is an unpleasant emotion, but is it therefore always
bad? The writer to the Hebrews says that Christ came to
deliver those *'who all their lives were held in slavery by their
fear of death'* (Hebrews 2:15). Yet the Psalmist cries: *'Fear the
LORD, you his saints, for those who fear him lack nothing'* (Psalm
34:9), and *'The fear of the LORD is pure, enduring forever'*
(Psalm 19:9).

Sorrow, in the same way, can be something that is good, or
it can be something that is bad.

Godly sorrow brings repentance that leads to salvation and leaves no regret, but worldly sorrow brings death.

(2 Corinthians 7:10)

We too readily make the assumption that all sorrow, unpleasant though it is, is good for us. Paul says that there is in fact a sorrow that produces death.

These examples are enough to establish this important conclusion:

▶ **the emotions are not of themselves reliable guides to behavior. We cannot rely on them to motivate us towards the good and away from the bad. Any specific emotion may, in fact, be either good or bad, right or wrong.**

Chapter 5

Where Did We Go Wrong?

In our emotions, human beings appear to have been equipped with very powerful but very unreliable motivators of behavior. This seems at first sight to confirm all we have read about the dangers of emotions, as far as our Christian life is concerned. Should we therefore ignore them, if not actively suppress them? The trouble is that neither ignoring nor suppressing emotions ever really succeeds. All that happens is that they are driven underground where they work just as powerfully as before, while we work out different reasons to justify our actions or attitudes.

The Christian who ignores or suppresses an emotional problem may acquire instead a set of intellectual or doctrinal difficulties. In fact, he is worse off than before. No argument, explanation or proof is ever likely to satisfy, because intellectual difficulties are not the real problem at all.

When we turn to the Scriptures, however, we discover that the emotions are unreliable not because God made them to be so, but because something has happened to them. It is part of the problem that entered with the Fall. Let us see what actually happened.

The person as originally created in God's image was a perfect and beautiful unity. In Adam, his mind ruled over his body, his spirit ruled over his mind, and the Holy Spirit ruled over his spirit. In this state he was a self-healing organism with no breach in his defenses through which sin or sickness or death could enter. Therefore, in their unfallen state, Adam

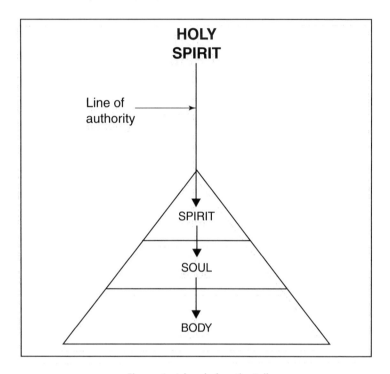

Figure 6: *Adam before the Fall*

and Eve were actually immortal; not that they could not die, but because there was no need for them to die. Death entered the human race by sin, as Paul points out in Romans 5:12.

Now, it was in the human soul that God had placed the functions of mind, emotions, and will. In the soul, therefore, lay the potential of free choice, and it was in this area that the devil launched his attack. To tempt Adam or Eve in their spirits would have been useless. The spirit (conscience) would simply have referred the matter to the Holy Spirit, and that would have been the end of it. But in the human soul-life lay the possibility of rebellion and self-assertion. It was here that the first human beings were tempted and it was here that they fell.

All of Eve's nature that was susceptible to arousal was appealed to. She saw that the tree was good for food (the bodily senses), it was a delight to the eyes (the emotions), and desirable to make one wise (the mind). So she took from its fruit and ate (the will). She gave the fruit to Adam also and he, not deceived as she was, also ate – and thus added spiritual rebellion to their sin.

From the Genesis account it is clear that the whole of human nature participated in sin, and the whole of human nature suffered from the Fall. As far as our emotions were concerned, the results were twofold:

1. **Perversion** A serious warping of our emotional reactions took place as far as moral judgement was concerned. This is immediately apparent. Towards a wholly good and loving God, Adam and Eve now have negative feelings that repel them from His presence. They are afraid and hide. Towards sin and disobedience they experience attractive feelings. There is no evidence on their part of reluctance towards eating the forbidden fruit. They succumb to the delight it promises.

   This is the fundamental flaw in our emotional nature today. Our feelings can no longer be relied upon to do what they were meant to do; that is, to motivate us towards the good and beautiful and in favor of a glorious, joyous fellowship with God.

2. **Disintegration** The whole human being was built around his spirit. It was through his spirit that he had contact with God, the source of life. Now sin has intervened and the human spirit is cut off from God. It does not cease to exist, but it falls into a powerless death state as in Figure 7.

The result is anarchy. Every part of human nature now strives for rule, or at least for autonomy. With some people it is the intellect that dominates: they seem almost unable to feel at all. At the other extreme there are those whose lives are ruled by their emotions which have run wild, today in a euphoria of excitement, tomorrow in the depths of depression.

Then there are people dominated by a very strong will. They thirst after power. Whatever they determine to do they

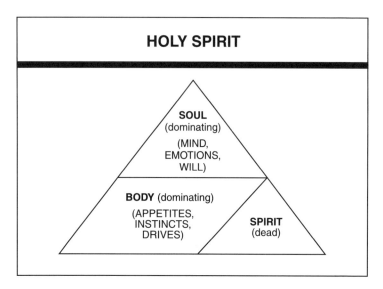

Figure 7: Fallen humanity

do, regardless of the cost to themselves or other people. And there are others who seem to be at the mercy of bodily appetites, which they are unable to control, but only to appease.

Lacking an integrating principle, fallen humanity is always under severe tension, in many cases coming apart at the seams. His mind pulls him one way, his feelings another. His bodily appetites seek satisfaction, his conscience condemns, his spirit cries out after a God his mind refuses to acknowledge, and so on. The result is unbearable inner strife. We even talk of people 'having a breakdown' under the stress. It is a good description of what actually happens.

. . . .

Chapter 6

Emotional Hurt

The need to respond to our environment emotionally, as well as physically or mentally, is part of the normal process of growing up. It follows that certain levels of emotional pressure and stimulus are as needful as physical effort. By no means all unpleasant emotional experiences are damaging. Grief, disappointment, failure, rejection and fear can all present us with opportunities to grow. If, however, the particular emotional trauma or stress is more than we can cope with at the time, critical hurt or damage can occur, often with long-lasting consequences.

In severe cases, a person's entire emotional response system can become disordered. There may be very strong emotional reactions without sufficient circumstances to warrant them. A fearful person can be afraid or anxious over trivial happenings, or even without knowing what he is afraid of or anxious about.

> *There they were, overwhelmed with dread,*
> *where there was nothing to dread.*   (Psalm 53:5)

Or the actual experience of feelings can be accompanied by excessive pain. The feelings associated with failure are unpleasant for anybody, but for some people they are so extremely painful as to be crippling.

> *My thoughts trouble me and I am distraught*
> *at the voice of the enemy,*
> *at the stares of the wicked;*

for they bring down suffering upon me
  and revile me in their anger.
My heart is in anguish within me;
  the terrors of death assail me.
Fear and trembling have beset me;
  horror has overwhelmed me.   (Psalm 55:2–5)

Not uncommonly, all feelings are repressed so that the person becomes apparently callous or apathetic. Often what has happened is that an emotional overload on a sensitive nature has, as it were, blown a fuse. After that, little feeling of any kind is experienced.

Evidences of emotional hurt

Wounds to the feelings are not visible in the same way as physical cuts and bruises, although they are just as real. In fact, the pain of emotional hurt is often more intense than that caused by physical injury or disease and is often the cause of sickness or accidents. The effects of emotional damage are generally observable in a person's behavior and attitudes, and some of the more common outward evidences of inner hurt need to be understood.

Firstly, there are great difficulties in the area of personal relationships. There may be domineering or possessive attitudes or, on the other hand, extreme dependency. Characteristically there is difficulty in giving and receiving real love and affection. This shows an inability to make friends or to keep friendships.

Secondly, there is often a very poor self-image or an inferiority complex. This comes out in many apparently contradictory ways: for example, excessive shyness, a very critical attitude towards others, a constant drive to prove oneself or be recognized, or an inordinate fear of failure.

Thirdly, there is a generally pessimistic outlook on life running all the way from negative talk and attitudes to compulsive thoughts of a gloomy or morbid nature and, in severe cases, to deep, depressive and suicidal states.

Finally, for the Christian with emotional problems, there

are often severe attacks of spiritual doubt and a loss of the assurance of salvation. It is very important in such cases to identify the real nature of the problem. Intellectual answers are to no avail because the real problem lies elsewhere.

Sources of inner hurt

As we have already seen, emotional wounds can be caused by traumatic emotional experiences that are beyond our capacity to handle at the time. Such experiences include bereavement, marriage breakdown, job failure, loss of health, accidents or loss of status or reputation.

Even more common sources of inner hurt come from living for long periods under conditions of stress such as domestic discord, nagging, criticism, heavy authoritarian discipline and other forms of psychological cruelty. There is a gradual accumulation of stress until sometimes the person reaches breaking point.

In other cases negative feelings, arising out of failure to attain goals that we see as able to meet our needs, can leave us with crippling feelings of worthlessness, guilt, resentment and anxiety.

When such experiences happen in childhood, it is often critical because of the extreme vulnerability of the personality in the early years. What Isaiah 53:2 expresses of Christ is also true of every child: *'He grew up before him like a tender shoot.'* Thus feelings of rejection in babyhood and early childhood can be devastating to some children, and can implant feelings of unconditional badness. A child can feel that he is totally worthless and deserving of only extreme punishment. I have spoken to many adults who have grown up like that.

I remember vividly one young married woman with great problems in her marriage and family. I learned that both she and her sister had been born illegitimate; later, when her mother married, the couple adopted this young woman's sister but never adopted her. She said: 'All my life I have felt a nothing, that only bad things ought to happen to me.' The tragedy is that what we expect from life we attract to us;

therefore, such lives are often marked with abnormal amounts of sickness, financial disasters, accidents and relational problems.

In marriage breakdowns children are often the innocent victims. Apart from the insecurity engendered by the break-up of the child's whole world, there is the trauma of finding that the two people the child loves the most are antagonistic towards one another. There is often an intense emotional involvement and sometimes the child, trying to resolve the clash of loyalties, blames himself as being the cause of the entire problem.

Sometimes the cause is not so much what the parents have done as what they have failed to do. For example, every person is born with two created needs: the need for love and the need for worth or significance. If these needs are not satisfied in childhood and in succeeding stages in our life, we will inevitably suffer.

But love needs to be experienced; and for it to be experienced, love has to be expressed towards us. Many adults, in talking to me about their childhood, have said: 'I know my parents loved me. They must have. But I guess I never felt it.' Parents need to express their love for their children – and do it often – both in words and actions.

The need for significance is not the same as the need for love. Certainly, the child who is aware of being loved has a better chance of feeling worthwhile, but that is not always the case. It is here that fathering is so important. One of the differences between fathering and mothering lies in the fact that, in very broad terms, the child looks to mother to meet his love needs, but looks to father to meet his need for significance. If a child falls and gets hurt, it is usually to mother that he turns for comfort; but if he comes home from school proud of something he has made, it is usually father he wants to show it to.

Parents can meet and over-meet a child's material needs; but if they fail to meet his needs for love or worth the possibility is that the child will grow up with feelings of rejection and inferiority that can cripple his emotional development.

Some important qualifications, however, need to be made in this area of childhood experience, otherwise parents can incur undeserved guilt about their performance as parents, and children can – quite wrongly – hold resentful feelings against parents.

The first is that the result of childhood experiences on a person's life is not completely predictable. It depends on the combined effect of the child's personality and his environment. Thus, what to one child may be a secure and encouraging home environment may be to another child, in the same family, stifling and repressive. What to one is a challenge to which they rise and through which they develop strength, is to another a daunting, even hopeless struggle. I have encountered people whose childhood was so horrifying I wondered how they had even survived as persons, yet they have come through almost unscathed. I have known others brought up in the most favorable conditions but one small incident has left them scarred for years.

The second is that what affects the child is how he interprets the situation, not what was the objective truth of the matter. Thus if a child interprets his father's attitude towards him as rejection or indifference it will affect him that way – even if he was entirely mistaken – and, in fact, his father loved him and was proud of him and expressed it as well as he could.

What happens in emotional hurt?

The most common result of inner hurt, particularly when it happens in childhood, is that emotional growth stops (see Figure 8). We say of such experiences, 'I never got over it.' It is a very accurate description of what happens. In some area of our feelings we fail to get past the problem experience. We are unable to integrate it or to respond to it and in that area it proves an insuperable hindrance to further growth. We may continue to grow up physically, intellectually, socially and even spiritually but certain parts of our emotional development are held back in a state of immaturity.

Figure 8: Inner hurt stops emotional growth

Feelings of inadequacy, anxiety and depression are often due to the fact that we are facing the demands and stresses of adult life while part of us is still feeling like a small child. Therefore, we feel that we cannot cope, or that we are never going to make it. Immaturity also comes out in some of our reactions to stress, for example temper tantrums, or in our inability to sacrifice short-term interests for long-term goals. A child has a very short time perspective; he lives very much in the immediate present. An emotionally immature adult often behaves in the same way.

God's desire for us, however, is maturity in every aspect of life:

> *Instead, speaking the truth in love, we will in all things grow up into him who is the Head, that is, Christ.*
>
> (Ephesians 4:15)

Chapter 7

Healing for Inner Hurt

We have seen repeatedly that God's answer to human need is always two-fold – the work of the cross and the work of the Holy Spirit. Now we have to see how this gracious provision also meets the need for healing of emotional hurt and pain.

The work of the cross

At Calvary, Jesus Christ as our Redeemer bore all the ruin that sin had brought on the human race. He suffered spiritually when He was made sin for us and bore the judgement of God on sin and evil. He suffered physically in one of the cruelest forms of execution fallen humanity has ever devised. In the ancient world crucifixion was the ultimate desecration inflicted on the dead bodies of fallen foes. It took the Romans to conceive of doing it while the victim was still alive.

Jesus also suffered emotionally; in fact, the biblical writers focus more on the shame of the cross than on its pain.

> *He was despised and rejected by men,*
> *a man of sorrows, and familiar with suffering.*
> *Like one from whom men hide their faces*
> *he was despised, and we esteemed him not.*
> *Surely he took up our infirmities*
> *and carried our sorrows,*
> *yet we considered him stricken by God,*
> *smitten by him, and afflicted.* (Isaiah 53:3–4)

Our Savior knew rejection and hurt beyond anything any other person has ever been called upon to bear. He came to His own beloved people, to His own beloved city and His own rejected Him in the name of the very Father He had come to reveal to them. On the cross Jesus was totally destroyed. He lost His dignity, He lost His reputation, He lost His following. Worse than all, as our sin-bearer, He was made sin for us. And then He had to find that in this hour of His greatest extremity His own Father had turned His back on Him. *'My God, my God, why have you forsaken me?'*

But because He suffered to the uttermost He is able to save us to the uttermost, therefore Peter can write triumphantly that *'by his wounds* [Greek *trauma*] *we are healed* [made whole again].*'

The work of the Spirit

In Romans 8:15 the Holy Spirit is called the Spirit of adoption. This is not adoption in our modern, western terms; adoption to the Jew was the entrance of the son into maturity and adulthood. The Holy Spirit is therefore the Spirit of maturity to enable us to grow up into Christ.

As part of this ministry He is also the one who binds up the broken heart:

> *The Spirit of the Sovereign* LORD *is on me,*
> *because the* LORD *has anointed me*
> *to preach good news to the poor.*
> *He has sent me to bind up the broken-hearted,*
> *to proclaim freedom for the captives*
> *and release from darkness for the prisoners . . .*
>
> (Isaiah 61:1)

The name that especially describes the ministry of the Holy Spirit is the one that Jesus gave him: the *Paraclete* or the Comforter. Let us see how he fulfills that ministry.

Chapter 8

The Process of Inner Healing

If you look forward to the diagram in Figure 22 (page 222), you will see that the link between the emotions and the human spirit is hope. In other words, for the Holy Spirit to heal our feelings He must gain access to them; we have to open up the hurt areas to His ministry.

Opening up the emotions

One of the most important points to remember in connection with inner healing is that **you can only deal with a feeling when you are feeling it**. Only then have we linked up directly with the hurt and can give God access to it. Look at Figure 9. If I have a problem with my will, for example a bad habit I need to break, I can only deal with it by an act of will because that is where the problem lies. No amount of reasoning (mind) or remorseful feelings (emotions) gets to grips with the real problem.

But when it comes to dealing with problems in the emotions, the usual response is to push the unpleasant feelings down and sometimes to bury them so that we no longer feel them. If we do pray about the problem, all we are in fact giving God is a mental report (+) from our mind, not the feeling (×) in our emotions.

I first learned this years ago, when I became aware that God wanted to touch something in my life but I didn't know what it was. One morning I woke up and remembered a dream I

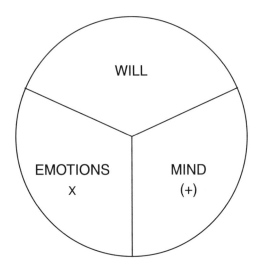

Figure 9: The human soul

had just had. The details of the dream are not important but its meaning was. What it showed me was that there was a path, if I could get on to it, that would lead me to the deep area that God wanted to reach. I lay in bed that morning, half-awake and half-asleep and said, 'Lord, how do I get on to that path?' Almost immediately the Lord spoke clearly into my mind, 'Start with childhood memories.'

Now, I have to say that this was long before I had read anything about inner healing or the healing of memories. It was years before anything appeared on such subjects, but immediately a memory flashed into my mind. It was something I hadn't consciously thought of for 25 years or more. I remembered being at high school in the middle years of the Depression of the 1930s. My family was very poor at the time so I could never afford soccer shoes or sports gear. But I was crazy about sports, so, if I wanted to play, I had to try to borrow someone else's shoes. I remembered that morning in bed how inferior and embarrassed and ashamed that used to make me feel.

Here is the important point. At that stage I just remembered the facts. But later the same day – it was a Saturday and

I was wallpapering a bedroom at the time – the whole thing came flooding back. But this time the feelings came with it. I felt the way I had felt as a Depression schoolboy, angry and ashamed and embarrassed. The feelings were so strong that I found myself crying all over a sheet of wallpaper. Then Jesus spoke to me, far more clearly than ever before, or since. I will never forget His words.

He said, 'I know how you feel. I was poor, too.'

When He said that, somehow He healed me. Something, that until then I had never been able to get over, was removed. His identification with my feelings healed a hurt I'd carried all those years, and the Holy Spirit bound up my broken heart.

I learned that morning to love some scriptures in a new way. 'Let the little children come to me, and do not hinder them...' (Matthew 19:14) I realized that though I was a grown man with a family, if part of me was feeling like a hurt child, I could come to Jesus as a hurt child and He would not reject me.

Only afterwards did I gradually become aware of how pervasive this buried hurt had been. For example, I always felt very tongue-tied and out of place among people who were well off, even though I was not by then poverty-stricken myself. I always had a terrible hassle buying things for myself – even things I could well afford. I now realize it was because I was still feeling like that little boy at school.

Remember also, that we are dealing with **present hurt**. Sometimes an expression like the 'healing of memories' can be a little misleading by suggesting that somehow we have to go back in time to change something that has already happened. The event that caused the hurt may, indeed, be years ago and memory is important, but the hurt is in the present and therefore accessible both to us and to God.

Because it is a present hurt, it is when I am feeling the hurt that I have linked up with the problem area. Part of our difficulty in dealing with childhood problems lies in the fact that we can no longer, as adults, identify with the way things appeared to us as children. Like Paul, we have become men and put away childish things. What, as adults, we look back at and laugh at, was often not a laughing matter at the time. When we tap into those still potent feelings, we soon discover this.

Sometimes we have no problem in opening up the emotions because our need is so urgent and overwhelming and the feelings so strong. At other times the surface feelings may not be the real problem but only the result of a deeper problem, or there may be long-practiced defense mechanisms at work to repress unwanted feelings. In these cases **we cannot open up the emotions by an act of will**. We can act only to stifle feelings; we cannot produce them. We cannot be joyful or angry or afraid at will. You can understand this if you have ever tried to laugh at a joke which you didn't get the point of, or tried to conjure up feelings of happiness while very depressed.

Memory is one of the most potent means of opening up the areas of hurt feelings. *'These things I remember as I pour out my soul . . . '* (Psalm 42:4). One of the peculiar qualities of emotional states is, as we have seen, that they can be triggered or re-activated by the memory of the situation that originally roused them.

But we need to allow the Holy Spirit to do the reminding. Only He knows which memories are significant – and they may not be the ones that we would think are important. We may have handled many stressful and even painful experiences entirely successfully and even profited from them. The critical experiences are the ones that were too much for us and have been buried out of mind. We therefore need to pray like David:

> *Search me, O God, and know my heart;*
> *   test me and know my anxious thoughts.'*   (Psalm 139:23)

In some cases, even the memory of the incident or the circumstances may be insufficient. We may recall the facts and still be unable to come to grips with the feelings. Often the blockage involves wrong attitudes that we have developed, and these have to be dealt with before healing is possible.

What often happens is that, after we have been hurt, resentment and bitterness come in. These have to be dealt with. While we are holding on to bitterness against those who have hurt us, we effectively lock Christ out of the situation. He cannot come in and heal us, no matter how much we ask Him, if by doing so it would seem to say that we have been right to harbor resentful thoughts against other people. Forgiveness is an essential prerequisite to healing.

Forgiveness is also important, because while we hold on to the unforgiveness we remain under the power of the person or situation responsible for our hurt. We are not free to choose how we will feel or react. We remain under the power of the hurt, even though the people concerned may be absent or even dead.

Forgiveness is not the same as pardon. In a sense, only God can pardon wrongdoing. When I forgive somebody who has wronged me, I am not saying that the wrong thing they did was right: I am dealing with my emotional reaction towards them. I am letting them go free from the grudges and hard feelings I have been holding against them. It is a matter of will. I hold things against them, therefore my will is involved; and therefore I can, by my free choice, release them from what I was holding against them. That is why forgiveness is a commandment: it begins with the choice of right behavior towards our enemies.

> *Love your enemies, do good to those who hate you, bless those who curse you, pray for those who ill-treat you.'*
> (Luke 6:27–28)

Grief or sorrow can also become a hindrance to healing. In a bereavement or a broken marriage or similar severed relationship, there is a grieving process through which we all must go. But it is possible for such a grief to become idolatrous if it becomes central to our heart, and our whole life begins to become organized around the memory of our loss. Such an idol has to be cast down.

Finally, we have to face the possibility that what we interpret as hurt may really come from our unwillingness or inability to face up to unpleasant truths about ourselves or our behavior. It is no good here trying to forgive the person who spoke the truth. He or she was in the right; we were in the wrong. Truth sometimes wounds, but truth wounds heal cleanly and quickly if we face up to them. An honest struggle with issues such as these almost always brings the real hurt and the real issues to the surface of our conscious awareness, so that they are accessible and we know what we are dealing with.

Handing over the hurt to Christ

Forgiveness is often a pre-requisite to healing, but forgiveness of itself will not heal us. In the same way it is necessary for the painful or negative feelings to be admitted to conscious awareness for us to deal with them; but that of itself will not make us whole. The hurt has to be handed over to Christ.

What makes gospel healing unique (and distinguishes it from all human psychotherapies) is that a real, living, supernatural Savior and Healer enters the picture. Often, with only an inkling of the suppressed pain and hurt that some people are holding at bay, I would be genuinely fearful of encouraging them to open up, if it were not for one thing – Jesus really is there.

Because He is there and because, when we are feeling the hurt, we have access to our hurt, we need to come to Him and hand it over. When we come to the end of our struggles with sin, we have learned to hand it over and be set free by supernatural grace. When we come to the end of our struggles to keep our pain below the threshold of consciousness, we have to hand it over to Him in the same way. The hurt and the pain can go off our hearts and into the blood of Jesus – in the same way as our sins and our sicknesses. The hurt we never thought we could get over, can go – permanently!

> *Trust in him at all times, O people;*
> *pour out your hearts to him,*
> *for God is our refuge.*   (Psalm 62:8)

When we hand over the hurt, we can receive in return the unconditional love of the Father to heal us. We are set free by the power of the Spirit of Adoption to begin to grow up out of our emotional immaturity.

Growing up into Christ

Because emotional hurt many times results in immaturity, the healing of the hurt involves a process of growth. In strict terms, you cannot be healed of immaturity or delivered from it: you can only grow out of it. Therefore, while the removal of the blockage or dealing with the inhibiting experience may take place in a moment, there is a time factor involved in the completion of the process. Because there is often a lot of life dammed up in these blocked-off areas, growth can take place very rapidly; but a period of time is always necessary.

We begin to experience the reality of God's love for us personally. I will never forget an experience I once had of the love of God. I had been asked, together with some Roman Catholic friends, to pray with a man who wanted to receive the baptism in the Holy Spirit. We spoke with him for a while on the subject and, although I had never met the brother before, I felt a real empathy and affection for him. Then he said, 'That's enough talking about it. Now pray for me.'

He knelt on the floor and we gathered around and began to pray for him. Suddenly I began to experience in my heart the way God loved that man. That night I discovered something about the love of God that I have never got over. I discovered that the love of God is not like human love at all. It is not human love enlarged or magnified many times. The difference is qualitative, not merely quantitative. I knew without a shadow of a doubt that even if that brother had got up off the floor and spat in my face, or even tried to kill me, it would not have affected that love one iota. I knew that.

The love of God is absolutely unconditioned and totally unconditional. It cannot be merited, earned, altered or lost – it just is. It reaches out to us whether we know it or not, whether we respond to or reject it. It was so amazing that, after we had stopped praying, I looked in my heart for that love; but it was not there any longer. I was back down to the level of human sympathy and affection.

That very same love reaches out to us all. We were made with the need for it. To me this experience explains why often our greatest longing for the presence of God comes not in times of need or distress, but in times of joy and happiness when, humanly speaking, life is at its fullest and best. In the midst of it all, something within us cries, 'Even this is not enough.'

That love – God's unconditional, eternal, infinite love – can make up any love deficit in any human life. Without it there will always be a love deficit.

Finally, God also gives us our significance. What brought an incredible sense of security into my life was when I learned that my worth, my eternal significance, is a total gift of God's grace. I cannot add one iota to it. If I succeed in everything I turn my hand to (and turn my hand to everything it is humanly possible to do), it does not add a scrap to my eternal worth. On the other hand, if I fail in everything I attempt and my whole life is a personal disaster, I do not diminish that eternal worth and value one scrap.

I may enjoy the approval of others and desire the sweet taste of success in achieving goals, but I do not need either of them to be eternally significant. Both hope and worth are God's gifts to His children.

Chapter 9

How to Live with Our Emotions

The full extent of the damage caused by sin needs to be understood, as this marks out for us the full scope of salvation. Salvation reaches every area affected by the Fall. Nothing has been left out. There is not only regeneration for the spirit; there is renewal for the mind and there is healing for the body; there is also release and harmony for the emotions.

One of the great truths regarding the cross of Christ, is that it is a work of reconciliation.

> *Once you were alienated from God and were enemies in your minds because of your evil behavior. But now he has reconciled you by Christ's physical body through death to present you holy in his sight, without blemish and free from accusation.* (Colossians 1:21–22)

Reconciliation is the bringing into harmony of two parties who were previously divided. On God's side it does not involve a change of feelings, because God's love for fallen human beings has never altered. But it does involve a change of relationship because God can now relate in blessing – and not in judgement – towards sinful human beings.

On the human side, our entire attitude towards God needs to be changed. Somehow our reactions of fear and guilt, rebellion, stubbornness and hardness have to be overcome:

> *...when we were God's enemies, we were reconciled to him*
> *through the death of his Son...*   (Romans 5:10)

How is God to reconcile a person who is His enemy? How do you go about reconciling someone who is hostile to you, and persists in holding on to his enmity? How is God to restore this disobedient person who runs away and hides, and who has all sorts of negative feelings every time God gets near? Look at God stretching out His hand all those years to Israel, while Israel repeatedly turned away and worshiped false and cruel idols.

Incarnation – the invasion

The first thing God had to do, if He was to change the attitude of the human race, was to get inside it. Only from inside could it be healed. This is why the incarnation is so important. The Eternal *Logos*, the Son, was made flesh. He took on Himself perfect humanity:

> *Since the children have flesh and blood, he too shared in*
> *their humanity ... For this reason he had to be made like his*
> *brothers in every way...*   (Hebrews 2:14, 17)

From all eternity the Persons in the Godhead have existed in a relationship of perfect love, or what John calls *'glory'* (John 17:5, 24). This love or glory has always been there in the Being of God. It was from this life that human beings by their sin have been cut off. God willed to Jesus, in His manhood, the extension of this love-relationship. In Jesus for the very first time a human being began to share the relationship of love and glory within the Godhead. It is expressed in several significant ways in the gospels. Jesus described it as being *'in the bosom of the Father'*, or being *'in heaven'*, or as reciprocal in-being – *'I am in the Father and the Father in me.'*

Now also, for the first time, a human being began to live life in total harmony and total fellowship and total obedience to God.

Baptism – the identification

Jesus did not come just to live one individual, perfect, human life before people. That might demonstrate the extent of our failure, but no more. He came to do much more than that. He came to change our relationship with God, and our attitude towards God. His baptism in the Jordan, at the hands of John the Baptist, was very significant. How are we to understand it? When we are baptized, we are baptized into union or identification with Christ. We identify with Him in His death, burial and resurrection. When Jesus was baptized He was baptized **into union with us**. That is, He identified Himself with our sinfulness, our lostness, and our alienation.

When we were baptized we enter into our vocation as saints, the called-out ones of God, the redeemed. When Jesus was baptized, He entered into His vocation as our redeemer. Thereafter, everything that Jesus did was directly associated with our salvation. He endured misunderstanding, spit, and hatred, not for Himself, but for us. He overcame temptation of every kind – not for Himself, but for our sakes. He lived a life of complete obedience to the will of the Father – for us, not for Himself. The struggle was always on the side of His humanity.

The question never was whether Satan could tempt or maim, or kill the eternal *Logos*. The question was whether Jesus, in His humanity, would overcome temptation and get through the cross on to resurrection ground. Had He failed, it would not have affected His divinity one iota – but we would have been lost for all eternity. Jesus had to get through as a human being in order to get us through.

Calvary – the incorporation

In John 12:32 Jesus said: *'But I, when I am lifted up from the earth, will draw all men to myself.'* John goes on to explain that He was saying this to indicate the kind of death He would die. It was to be a dying not only in the place of humanity, but a dying that gave humanity a part in that same experience. Paul has the same understanding in Galatians 2:20:

'I have been crucified with Christ...' It is not just a question of dealing with our guilt. It is a question of reconciliation, of restoring a broken relationship, and changing ingrained attitudes of fear and hostility.

▶ **Jesus' humanity became on the cross a corporate humanity, which embraced all who would believe in Him, so that through His dying and resurrection they would be brought into the same relationship with God which He enjoyed.**

In Ephesians 2:5–6 Paul works this out in detail. We are not only crucified in Christ, we are raised up with Him. We are not only raised up with Him, we are placed with Him in heavenly places. What are these heavenly places? They are the relationship with the Father and the Son, and the Holy Spirit; it is the relationship of 'in-being' that Jesus experienced: the Father in Him, and He in the Father. Now the Father is in us, and we are in the Father; the Son is in us, and we are in Christ; the Holy Spirit is in us and we are in the Spirit.

This is reconciliation. Out of it springs a changed attitude towards God. Now our emotional reactions towards Him are no longer fear, guilt and hostility but –

> *Though you have not seen him, you love him; and even though you do not see him now, you believe in him and are filled with an inexpressible and glorious joy...* (1 Peter 1:8)

Furthermore, human nature is brought back into harmony with the original design.

God's eternal intention for humanity was always that we should become children of God through Christ (Ephesians 1:5). His purpose in redemption is that people *'be conformed to the likeness of his Son'* (Romans 8:29). Therefore Jesus became a prototype of the reconciled order of humanity. In Him every part of the human personality is brought into its rightful place, into the harmony that marks all God's creative work.

Let us see what this means for us in the area of our emotional life:

First, the emotions are purified. *'Create in me a pure heart, O God...'* cries the psalmist (Psalm 51:10). In the Bible the heart generally refers to the seat of the emotions. Acts 15:9 tells us that God cleanses the heart by faith. The emotions can be cleansed from the perversion caused by sin, so that they can become what they were intended to be: powerful motivators towards the good, and away from the bad. Did you think it would ever be possible for you to trust your feelings? To rely on them to motivate you towards God?

> *As the deer pants for streams of water,*
> *so my soul pants for you, O God.*
> *My soul thirsts for God, for the living God.* (Psalm 42:1–2)

> *Your statutes are my heritage forever;*
> *they are the joy of my life...*
> *I hate double-minded men,*
> *but I love your law.* (Psalm 119:111, 113)

Secondly, the emotions can be released. The problem with many people is not too much feeling, but too little. I find more people with an emotional temperature that is too low, than one that is too high. For many, many people the natural expression of affection and emotion has been almost totally inhibited.

There is a wonderful promise in Ezekiel 36:26 that is part of the new covenant in Christ. We usually miss its real significance:

> *I will give you a new heart and put a new spirit in you; I will remove from you your heart of stone and give you a heart of flesh.* (Ezekiel 36:23)

Part of our rights under the new covenant is to receive for our stony lack of feelings a heart of flesh. In other words, we can have the affective side of our nature released and a new set of emotions imparted. Does that seem too good to be true?

Not only do we have the **life** of Christ within us, but 1 Corinthians 2:16 tells us that we have the **mind** of Christ.

Not only do we have the mind of Christ, but Philippians 1:8 tells us that we have the **affections** of Christ. Paul says, '*God can testify how I long for all of you with the affection of Christ Jesus.*' That is the new heart that the prophet is speaking about. Would you like to have the Lord take out of your life your inhibited, stony heart and give you His own emotional responses? Because He has already promised to do so you can receive the new heart, the new affections that are your covenant rights in Christ.

I once met a young man who suffered from the problem of a stony heart. His father had just died, but what frightened the young man was the discovery that he felt nothing at all. No loss, no grief, no love – nothing. He then became aware of the fact that there was the same absence of feeling towards his wife, and his two small children. He could show no affection whatsoever towards them, although he treated them well enough externally. When I met him, he was being treated by a psychiatrist, but was conscious that he was making no real progress.

That young man and his wife came to a small weekend retreat we were having. One night he opened his heart to the Lord, and received Jesus as his savior. Do you know what happened? The Lord took away his stony heart and gave him a new heart. He wept until I thought the floor of the little cabin would be awash with tears. Often afterwards he used to come back, and tell me how his life had changed. Now he could tickle his small children to make them laugh, and could pick them up, fondle them, and love them. It is a beautiful thing to see someone come alive like that.

Jesus said,

> The thief comes only to steal and kill and destroy; I have come that they may have life, and have it to the full.'
>
> (John 10:10)

▶ **In the reconciled personality it becomes safe for the emotions to be released, to fulfill their proper function, because God has restored, in Christ, life to the human spirit.**

We have seen that the human personality was built around our spirit as the integrating factor. This was to be the central principle that held everything in place and everything in harmony, and linked us securely to God, the source of our life. When sin entered, the spirit lost its place of authority. Disharmony, dis-ease, and disintegration followed. There is a great deal of emphasis today on freedom, but freedom that resides solely and autonomously in the human will is almost totally destructive. Such freedom demands that whatever a person is capable of doing, he must be allowed to do. No restraints, moral or otherwise can stand in the way.

However, the created center for our being was not our free will, but our spirit; and as we have seen, each function of the spirit is related to a function of the soul. Specifically the spiritual function of communication is intended to rule over the emotions.

We sometimes use a diagram as in Figure 10 to illustrate the relationship between body, soul and spirit. It is quite a useful model and is, in fact, the way most of us are accustomed to live. But notice what the consequences are as far as the emotions are concerned.

1. A stimulus of one sort or another reaches us through the senses. Let us imagine it is the sight of a neighbor with whom we had a row last week. We have the stimulus: the neighbor A, and our physical perception B: we see the neighbor.

2. From this sensory perception (the sight of the neighbor), an emotional response is activated. It may be irritation, embarrassment, anger or resentment. We remember what he said, and the way he said it, what we should have said in return, but didn't think of in time, and so on.

3. Finally, with all these emotions in full spate, our spirit, functioning as conscience, intervenes and passes judgment on our behavior. 'That is wrong. You should not be angry or resentful towards your neighbor.'

The problem is that the conscience has to deal with emotions that are already aroused. It is at this point of

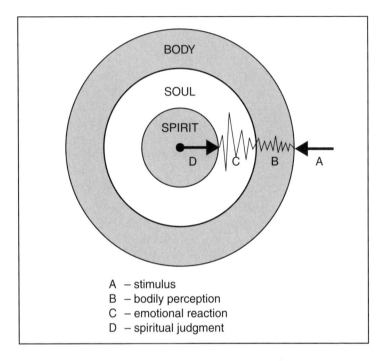

Figure 10: Body soul and spirit – the emotional responses

action that the influence of the conscience tends to be weakest.

When you turn to the gospels, you find that Jesus did not live this way at all. What we consider as natural is, in fact, **inverted**. To come into proper balance, it needs to be **converted**.

I discovered that, in terms of relationship to people, to situations, and to the environment, Jesus lived with His spirit on the outside. If you look at Figure 11, you will see what is meant. Actually this model corresponds better to the extent of our reach. Physically, our senses reach out a few feet, as far as touch is concerned; a few yards as far as hearing is concerned; a few miles as far as sight is concerned. The reach of our mind is vastly greater. The reach of our spirit is right out into eternity, into the infinite, into God.

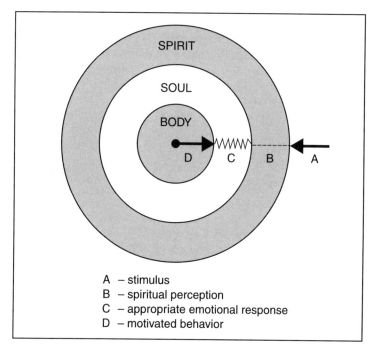

Figure 11: Spirit, soul and body in the experience of Jesus

Because Jesus lived with His spirit out front, as it were, it meant that He touched situations spiritually first. Therefore the emotional responses that motivated His actions arose out of spiritual perceptions.

This is so important that we need to establish it from the gospel records.

Take the account in Mark chapter 6. A great crowd had seen Jesus going off in a boat with His disciples, and ran ahead to wait for Him.

When Jesus landed and saw a large crowd, he had compassion on them, because they were like sheep without a shepherd. So he began teaching them many things. (Mark 6:34)

What happened? Jesus 'saw' them. It means He saw them with insight. He did not just observe a crowd of men, women and children. He had a spiritual comprehension of what they really were like: sheep with no one to care for them.

Out of this spiritual comprehension there came an emotional response – compassion. From this compassionate motivation there came the appropriate action – He began to teach them, and later to feed them.

Take a different example, recorded in Mark 3. Jesus goes into the synagogue and finds a man there with a withered hand. He said to the assembled congregation, *'Which is lawful on the Sabbath: to do good or to do evil, to save life or to kill?'*

They kept silent. It might appear to us that they just didn't know the answer.

> *He looked round at them in anger and, deeply distressed at their stubborn hearts, said to the man, 'Stretch out your hand.' He stretched it out, and his hand was completely restored.* (Mark 3:5)

What Jesus saw when He looked around, was the hard, bitter hearts of those who would rather see a man stay crippled than have their religious rules broken. Out of that spiritual knowledge came an emotional response, in this case grief, and anger. From the motivation of these feelings Jesus calls the crippled man out and in their presence – and on the Sabbath day – He heals the withered hand.

One final illustration. In Luke chapter 19, Jesus has entered Jerusalem and the crowds have cast their garments in the roadway, welcoming him with cries of 'Hosanna!'

> *As he approached Jerusalem and saw the city, he wept over it and said, 'If you, even you, had only known on this day what would bring you peace – but now it is hidden from your eyes. The days will come upon you when your enemies will build an embankment against you and encircle you and hem you in on every side . . . '* (Luke 19:41–43)

Jesus saw the city. He saw more than just the streets, buildings and geographical layout. The spirit of prophecy came on Him, and He 'saw' the state of the city and the outworking of its sin. And He wept for the grief of it, even as He pronounced its inevitable judgement.

In each of these cases the succession of events is the same:

1. a spiritual contact or apprehension;
2. from that, an emotional reaction;
3. out of that, an appropriate action.

Emotion and perception

The important principle that is being illustrated here is that emotions depend largely on perceptions. Our feelings are aroused by the way in which we interpret situations and events. For example, there is a thunderous crash at 3 o'clock in the morning and you sit bolt upright in bed, your heart pounding and your eyes popping out of your head. Burglars . . . an earthquake . . . the Rapture . . . a plane crash? Then the light goes on, and you discover your husband has lost his way in the dark and fallen over the chest. Now you feel amusement, commiseration or irritation depending on how often he is in the habit of doing this kind of thing, and how happy your relationship is at the moment. Same stimulus: different perceptions, different emotions.

The physical sensations you will experience in jumping off a dock to go for a swim on a hot day are very similar to those you will experience if you accidentally fall off a dock when bidding farewell to some friends. Your emotional reactions will be very different because your perceptions are different.

Jesus' emotional reactions were wholly appropriate in every circumstance because His perception was true. His perception of situations was always true because He perceived with His spirit. Hear Him explain the same way of living in John 5:30:

> *By myself I can do nothing; I judge only as I hear, and my judgement is just, for I seek not to please myself but him who sent me.*

Jesus never judged according to the outward look of circumstances. He judged as He 'heard', that is, by the inner witness of His spirit.

The practical question, of course, is: how do we begin to live in this 'inside-out' (that is really right-side-out) kind of way? How are we, for our part, to begin to live towards life so that we touch people and situations with our spirit alert, to see them the way Jesus sees them, and feel towards them with His affections?

When we learn to perceive with our spirit, then our emotional responses will reflect truth and reality in a more accurate way. They will thus become more dependable, and more reliable motivators of behavior.

Most of us have learned to live quite differently. Instead of projecting towards people or situations our real self, we project an image or façade that we think will be acceptable. This image is fairly expendable because there is not very much of our real self invested in it. Thus, if it is rejected, we are not too troubled. Other people project similar images towards us, and we in turn react to their behavior. We seldom seem to get near the real person that lies behind the behavior, so the possibilities for misunderstanding are legion.

We must learn to live in an open way towards people and situations, so that our real self is invested in everything we do or say. If people respond in the same way, we will perceive the true reality that is there. Even if they do not, we will often detect behind the façade that is presented, the true self – frightened, anxious or wary – that would like to respond, but dare not. We will find ourselves reacting spontaneously in a compassionate and understanding way to the real person, and not the image.

Here are the important steps to get started on this new style of living:

1. We can learn to live in this way first of all towards the Lord. He totally accepts us, and is totally responsive to us. David had learned the security of this kind of openness before God:

> *Search me, O God, and know my heart;*
> *test me and know my anxious thoughts.*
> *See if there is any offensive way in me,*
> *and lead me in the way everlasting.*
>
> (Psalm 139:23–24)

We cannot hide from Him. We do not need to hide from Him, because we are totally accepted in His love.

2. We need the Lord to sanctify us by His Holy Spirit so that we can live confidently and spontaneously out of our spirit. Unless it is cleansed, what can come out is not likely to bring a response of life. We have to live out of the new self, created in Christ Jesus *'in true righteousness and holiness'* (Ephesians 4:24).

3. We need to become aware of the times when we are not living out of the new self, or out of the spirit. I remember once going to a Catholic charismatic prayer meeting. As I went in, a young man I had never met before came up, put his arms around me, and gave me a real, warm, loving hug. I put my arms around him, when suddenly I became painfully aware that he was loving me, but all I was doing was putting my arms around him. I was holding my heart back, because I was among new people.

   I am learning to discern those times when I slip back into projecting a hollow image, and I am becoming increasingly uncomfortable with the falsity of it. Truth – or reality – is a very freeing thing.

4. When we learn to live out towards people and situations in this way, we not only perceive truth more clearly, but we make a way for the Holy Spirit to reach out of our personality to touch others. Jesus said in John 7:38, *'streams of living water will flow from within him.'* The streams cannot flow if our innermost being is shut up in safety, and we project a false, sham image. The Spirit of truth, the Spirit of reality, can find no way to use a falsehood. No matter how inept or inadequate we may feel, our true inner being provides the Spirit with all that He needs to flow out as a river of life. When this

happens, we experience not our feelings, but the feelings of the Holy Spirit. If this seems too much to grasp, listen to Paul again:

> *God can testify how I long for all of you with the affection of Christ Jesus.*   (Philippians 1:8)

PART III

Chapter 10

The Freedom of the Will

For a long time, even after I learned that salvation is more than just forgiveness, I still thought that there was one area of our lives in which God had to leave us to struggle on our own: the realm of the human will. I knew that there was renewal for the mind and release for the emotions, but I could not see how God could intervene to help in the realm of the will without interfering with my essential moral freedom.

Yet I also knew that the will was the area of my greatest need. How could I become truly obedient to the will of God? Even if I succeeded today, was there any real hope that I could depend on myself to remain obedient tomorrow?

It seemed that I was doomed to be like a parent in charge of an incorrigibly willful and disobedient child, who could never be trusted to behave properly unless someone was standing over him all the time.

Reading Romans chapter 7 seemed to confirm my worst suspicions:

> *I do not understand what I do. For what I want to do I do not do, but what I hate I do.* (Romans 7:15)

Paul, it seemed, was stuck with the very same problem ... in fact, he appeared to go to some pains to hammer the lid securely on the coffin.

...the sinful mind [or the flesh] *is hostile to God. It does not submit to God's law, nor can it do so.*

(Romans 8:7)

True, he spoke of being 'crucified with Christ', and of 'counting ourselves dead to sin but alive to God in Christ Jesus', as somehow being the answer to the problem; but that raised other issues as well. If it so happened that we could go through such an experience to become like Paul, Christ's bond-slave, what were we then left with: freedom or merely an illusion of freedom? Perhaps the Bible said that we were free, but all the time we knew – and God knew – that we were not really free at all. We had yielded up our will so, although we might even feel free, God had a secret rope around our ankles all the time and could pull us into line any time we strayed!

And then I began to learn something that has never ceased to excite me: God, I discovered, has a great stake in our freedom. He has gone to infinite lengths to set us free; and all His purposes with us require that we remain free. We need to see why this is so.

Firstly, God is love. Because that is His nature, our relationship with Him is founded on love and trust.

Secondly, for love and trust to exist at all, there must be the free choice of a free will.

This is true even on the human level. John loves Jane and is desperately anxious for Jane to love him in return. But John knows that her response is only genuine love if it is free. If he could somehow 'zap' her, or condition her so that she had to love him, he knows that it would be no good. In other words, John has to take the risk of leaving Jane free so that she can freely reject him or freely respond to him. Only then is love possible.

God knows this far better than us because He is Love itself, and He desires to have people relating to Him only on that basis. Therefore, in all His dealings with us, before and after we are born again, He has left the human will free.

We will have to return to this more than once because it is of vital importance, but first of all let us discover some basic facts that we need to know about the will itself and what we mean by the concept of freedom.

The human will – a choosing mechanism

One important aspect of our human uniqueness among God's creatures is the area of choice that has been entrusted to us. True, animals make certain choices, but their choices are locked into patterns of behavior that are essentially instinctive. They are part of the adaptive response of the animal to its environment.

We are different. God, the uncreated Creator, making people in His own image and after His own likeness, made each of us a created creator. That is, we can make choices that are creative. We can choose our own goals. We can decide what we will become.

The behavior of an animal can be changed or modified by conditioning. It can learn. A horse can be broken to the saddle and a puppy can be house-trained. Only human beings, however, can make moral choices, that is decisions of our will that are based, not on instinct or conditioning, but on values or standards of right and wrong.

Therefore only human beings can sin. A parrot may say, 'Sunny day, sunny day', when in fact, it is pouring with rain – yet it could not be said to be telling lies. A dog may run off with my slipper but it is not stealing. Only people have the freedom of choice that makes moral behavior or misbehavior possible.

The choosing part of the soul that finally makes these choices is the will. It is the final step in the process that results in human behavior. We can illustrate the whole process in terms of a motor vehicle:

- The mind, like the steering wheel, is the directing mechanism.
- The emotions are, like the motor, the driving or motivating mechanism.
- The will is the clutch, the choosing or engaging mechanism.

All three must function in harmony to produce effective behavior. A decision to do something – but without adequate motivation – is likely to stall, like letting the clutch out with the engine merely idling. Extreme emotional drives – terror, for example – can overwhelm the rational faculties and produce the disorganized behavior of panic states. It is rather like driving off with the accelerator down to the floor and both hands off the steering wheel! And the person who is wildly enthusiastic about some idea but never actually does anything about it is like the new student driver, with the engine roaring, the wheel firmly gripped in both hands – and the gears in neutral.

This principle of total response is fundamental in all our relationships, both with God and other people. It is what Jesus meant when He spoke of *'all your heart, all your mind, all your soul and all your strength.'* If we do not grasp this we will seriously misunderstand many of the basic concepts of the Bible such as repentance, faith, love, and so on. Each of these requires a response from mind **and** feelings **and** will. If the response is from only one of these areas, we end up with something quite different like this:

	If it is only reason is –	If it is only feelings is –	If it is only will is –
Repentance	opinion-change	remorse	reformation
Faith	belief	impulse	determination
Love	admiration	sentiment	charity

Nevertheless, it is most often in the area of the will that our response breaks down, so that repentance never gets beyond a change of opinion or feelings of remorse, and faith remains mere impulse or mental assent. We must therefore see the basic nature of the problem with human will.

The nature of free will

There is a lot of talk today about freedom. There is also an uneasy feeling that, although we are more vocal about it, in actual fact the area of real human freedom is dwindling rapidly and may, in our modern 'managed' society, have all but disappeared.

We must, however, be perfectly clear as to the nature of human freedom. Freedom is **not** the central principle of human life and it is **not** absolute. The French philosopher, Jean Paul Sartre, saw quite clearly what happens when human freedom is made an absolute. He says it will lead inevitably to three things – deicide (the killing of God), murder, and suicide. See what this means.

God is the ultimate limit to human moral freedom. Today, whatever people can do, they want to be free to do – whether it is genetic engineering or the development of horrendous methods of mass nuclear destruction. But concerning some of the things which modern humanity can do because we have the technological capacity, God still says, *'You shall not...'* Therefore, if a person is to be 'free', God must be considered dead.

Then, if I am to be fully free to do whatever I like, your existence becomes a potential limitation on that freedom. So I must kill you to express total human freedom and my refusal to be fettered by any limitation. Freedom leads to murder.

Even that is not the end. My own existence then becomes a limiting factor, so that to attain ultimate authentic freedom I must be free to transcend my own being – in other words, to kill myself.

Here is the full disclosure of Satan's intention in the Garden of Eden when he tempted the first people to snatch their 'freedom' and become as God.

He was a murderer from the beginning. (John 8:44)

The truth about freedom

What, then, is the truth about human freedom? It is this:

▶ **Freedom must always be expressed within the limits laid down by law.**

We call this obedience.

Disobedience, or flouting the law, means that the law becomes our enemy and we are no longer free.

The principle is clearly seen in the operation of the natural laws. I am not 'free' to walk up the vertical side of a city building in defiance of the law of gravity. If I try to do so, the law becomes my enemy and lands me flat on my back on the pavement.

It is the same with the laws that govern society. The lawbreaker loses his freedom. Even if he is not apprehended, he has lost the inner freedom to walk down the street without being concerned whether his misdemeanors are about to catch up with him.

The moral and spiritual laws built into the universe work just the same way. If I break them, they turn against me – as devastatingly and inexorably as any other law, natural or man-made. Today we no longer doubt this. We are reaping the consequences of generations of lawbreaking, and the result is waste, pollution, want, misery, illness, and death.

The limitations of law, we shall find, can be transcended in only one way: by obeying a higher law that operates in the same realm. I can overcome the law of gravity, not by defying it, but by submitting to a higher law. In other words, I step into an elevator or board an aircraft. But my response is still obedience – the recognition of law. We will return to this aspect later on.

Chapter 11

The Power Struggle
in the Universe

The Bible reveals that the universe is the scene of a great power struggle between God and Satan. What is more, in this struggle human beings play a strategic part. We ourselves are, in fact, the main battleground. But we must understand clearly that it is not a struggle of naked power. It is not to find out whether God is more powerful than Satan. (I meet many Christians who believe that God is stronger than Satan – but only just. They are relieved to read the end of the Bible and find that we win – seemingly by a narrow margin!) It is not like that at all. There never has been any question as to whether God is stronger than Satan, or whether God could blot out Satan any time He chooses, without even having to stir a little finger. When it comes to a question of naked power, there is no competition with omnipotence!

The conflict in the universe is over something quite different. It is a moral and spiritual struggle.

The question at stake is whether God or Satan will win our obedient response and our allegiance. In this struggle God has, in fact, allowed the scales to be weighted against Him to an incredible degree. The response God seeks from us is nothing less than love. Therefore He must take the risk, as we said before, of allowing human beings a free and unforced response. Satan has no such scruples. He will use deception, lies, trickery, pressure, compulsion, perversion and anything that suits his purpose. Anything but free, unfettered choice – that he cannot risk.

The rival laws

In the book of Romans, the apostle Paul describes this conflict very clearly in terms of two rival laws competing for our obedience. The question of obedience is, as we have seen elsewhere, the crucial issue.

> *Don't you know that when you offer yourselves to someone to obey him as slaves, you are slaves to the one whom you obey – whether you are slaves to sin, which leads to death, or to obedience, which leads to righteousness?*   (Romans 6:16)

The rival laws which thus seek our obedience are set out in Romans 8:2. They are the law of God, and the law of sin and death.

The law of God

Understand that the law of God is not something God made up: it is the way God is. The law is the expression of God's character. Therefore the law is holy and righteous and good. Sometimes we draw a wrong and completely unbiblical contrast between grace and law, as though grace is good but law is bad. That is not true.

The law of God is the law of unselfish love. It is the expression of the wonderful character of God and it is the way that God chooses to live. David understood this. Psalm 119 is one long rhapsody of a man who knew law as a revelation of God:

> *The law from your mouth is more precious to me*
> *   than thousands of pieces of silver and gold...*
> *How sweet are your words to my taste,*
> *   sweeter than honey to my mouth!...*
> *Your promises have been thoroughly tested,*
> *   and your servant loves them...*
> *I will walk about in freedom,*
> *   for I have sought out your precepts.*
>   (Psalm 119:72, 103, 140, 45)

The law of sin and death

Just as the law of God is the way God is, so the law of sin and death is the way Satan is. In other words, it is the expression of the devil's character. Jesus said that Satan was a murderer and a liar from the beginning; he comes only to kill and to steal and to destroy. Therefore we must not be surprised if his law produces the same fruits.

The appeal of sin is founded on deception and delusion. Its end is hidden. Only the Bible reveals the truth about its end.

> *There is a way that seems right to a man,*
> *but in the end it leads to death.* (Proverbs 14:12)

Law and the claim to authority

We now have to see how these competing laws lay claim to human obedience. This section may not seem easy, but it needs to be followed carefully. Once understood, the whole concept of freedom and obedience will be seen in its true perspective.

1. Law demands our obedience on the basis of the authority that it claims

In other words there is an 'ought-ness' about the demand of law that is quite different from the question of liking or preference. Law expects that we 'ought' to do what it demands, whether we want to or not. It does so because it claims to be authoritative.

We understand this clearly as far as the law of God is concerned. We may reject its demands, but we know while we are doing so that we are disobeying an authority that lays claim to our obedience.

With the law of sin and death we are often deceived. Sin is presented to us as a matter of choice or preference. We imagine we can take it or leave it. Only later, when we try to break free, do we come up against its imperious demand: we become conscious of its operation as law.

*...I see another law at work in the members of my body,
waging war against the law of my mind and making me a
prisoner of the law of sin at work within my members.*

(Romans 7:23)

What, then, is the basis for law's claim to be authoritative?
What are the grounds on which it demands my obedience?
Let us examine this question of authority.

2. Authority is power that we recognize as being legitimate

I am driving along the street in my car and a woman dressed
in a particular manner steps out into the road and holds up
her hand. Obediently I slow down and stop. Why do I do so?
Not because she is so big that she could physically obstruct
the passage of my car, but because from her uniform I see
that she is a police officer and thus represents a power that I
recognize as legitimate.

In other words, the question of obedience or disobedience
only arises when I am faced with authority, and that authority exists for me only if the power it represents is one that I
recognize as being legitimate.

But it now seems we must go further back still. How, in
fact, do I decide whether power is legitimate or not? This is
the important step.

3. I recognize power as being legitimate when the norms (or standards) that it represents correspond with my inner value system

Suppose I am in Russia, and in the small hours of the
morning some uniformed police officers knock on my door
and begin talking ominously about salt mines in Siberia.
What would my reaction be? Apart from understandable fear,
I would be likely to regard such power as tyrannical and
oppressive and an illegitimate exercise of force. Why? They
are policemen just the same as those at home. They, too, may
direct traffic, control football crowds and track down crim-
inals, just like the police in my own country.

Nevertheless I would be likely to regard the actions of my uninvited visitors as an illegitimate exercise of power. This is because the norms which that police force represents – the absolute power of the state – do not correspond with my inner set of values which are those of democratic freedom and the rights of the individual.

In other words, we do not recognize as legitimate any exercise of power that is at variance with our inner value system. We may have to comply with such laws and regulations, but we will do so reluctantly, grudgingly and with a feeling that it is wrong and unfair. If we can find a way around the law, we are likely to feel justified rather than have a bad conscience about it. In other words, even if we conform, we do not obey.

External law and inner values

We come now to a principle that is of extreme importance to this whole issue, and one that needs to be grasped by every parent. It is this:

▶ **When external law and inner values are in conflict, inner values will, in the long run, win out every time.**

A child growing up in a family is learning two quite distinct things. Consciously he is learning from his parents a set of rules regarding what is right and what is wrong behavior – share your toys, don't tell lies, be obedient to Mommy and Daddy, brush your teeth after meals, and so on.

Unconsciously, but just as surely, he is learning a set of values: the value system by which his parents live.

When these two – the code of behavioral rules and the value system by which the parents actually live – are inconsistent or at variance with each other, child as well as parents are in trouble.

For example, little Jason has just told a lie and been found out. He is about to be punished for it so that he can learn that he is not to tell lies. Just then there is a knock at the front door. Mother groans in dismay and says, 'Oh, it's that awful Mrs Smith. Jason, go and tell her I've had to go out.'

Jason learns two things. He learns that a lie is 'an abomination to the Lord,' but he also learns that it is a 'very present help in time of trouble'! In other words, he learns that you shouldn't lie, but that if you are as big as Mom or Dad so that no one can smack you, you can tell lies when it is a convenient way of getting out of trouble.

This is why you get parents who tell you, 'Jason is a good little boy at home, but I can't trust him out of my sight.' When Jason is within reach of mother's hand and eye, prudence and past experience may dictate that he conforms to the required standards of behavior. But when he is on his own, the external standards of behavior that his parents have set for him soon lose out against the inner values he has also acquired, and he pleases himself in much the same way as his parents do.

Israel, Egypt and the ten commandments

We can see an even better illustration of the same principle in God's dealings with Israel in the Old Testament. The whole history of these centuries can be seen as a conflict between external law and inner values. It was, in one way, not very difficult for God to get Israel out of Egypt. It depended on His power and that was more than adequate. Over four hundred years' residence in Egypt had caused the people to acquire a set of Egyptian inner values.

All through the wilderness those values were there. Continually they surfaced to draw the people back to Egypt, even though Egypt meant slavery and bondage. The memory of the leeks and onions and the garlic of Egypt made them turn up their noses at the manna, angels' food though it was.

When the nation reached the land of Canaan it was the same. As long as judges or prophets ruled, or kings were righteous and godly men, the nation obeyed the law and served their Covenant God. But between times, with uncanny regularity, the people reverted to pagan ways. Temple worship was neglected; the law was unread; the idols and all the dark perversions of occult religion reappeared.

Even in times of apparent faithfulness, outward conformity is far from being obedience, and this the prophets saw with increasing clarity:

> *The LORD says:*
> *'These people come near to me with their mouth*
>   *and honor me with their lips,*
>   *but their hearts are far from me.*
> *Their worship of me*
>   *is made up only of rules taught by men.'*   (Isaiah 29:13)

But this is not only Israel's problem. It is also the problem of the whole human race.

The origins of the flesh

We can now begin to see the real shape of the problem that Paul saw in human nature.

Through Adam's initial disobedience, sin entered into the world, and with sin came death. Not only Adam but all people since, have sinned, so that the entire human race has fallen under the law of sin and death. Furthermore this subservience to the law of sin and death has made humanity the bond-slave of Satan, so by our nature we follow *'... the ways of this world and of the ruler of the kingdom of the air, the spirit who is now at work in those who are disobedient'* (Ephesians 2:2).

The prince of the power of the air is Satan, who now has access to the inner nature of a person. He has used that access to implant in human hearts a set of inner values. *'Above all else, guard your heart'*, says Proverbs 4:23, *'for it is the wellspring of life.'*

What flows from the inner springs of fallen humanity is the value system that Satan has planted there. It is what the New Testament calls *'the flesh'* or *'the fallen nature'*, or *'this body of sin and death'*. Its origin, its relationships and its authority are clearly seen in Figure 12.

It is important to realize that by 'the flesh' the Bible does not here mean the body. The body is not evil. Christianity is,

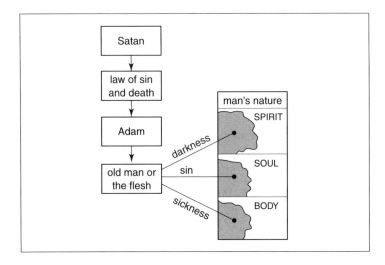

Figure 12: Origins and influence of the flesh

in fact, the only religion that has a proper view of the human body. It is a very exalted view. The believer's body is *'a temple of the Holy Spirit'*, its parts are *'members of Christ himself'* (1 Corinthians 6:19, 15), we are to present our bodies *'as living sacrifices, holy and pleasing to God'* (Romans 12:1), and one day they will be *'clothed with immortality'* (1 Corinthians 15:53).

The flesh, however, refers to the sinful principle of self-gratification that holds human nature in bondage to the law of sin and death. The flesh, in fact, has a destructive influence on the whole of tripartite human nature:

- It brings darkness to his spirit.
- It brings sin to his soul.
- It brings sickness to his body.

The inner values of the flesh are detailed in Galatians 5:19–21:

> *The acts of the sinful nature are obvious: sexual immorality, impurity and debauchery; idolatry and witchcraft; hatred, discord, jealousy, fits of rage, selfish ambition, dissentions,*

factions and envy; drunkenness, orgies, and the like. I warn you, as I did before, that those who live like this will not inherit the kingdom of God.

The flesh and the rival laws

If a person has these inner values, we can see what his attitude will be to the law of God. He will reject its authority and deny its legitimacy, because its norms are totally at variance with his fleshly inner values. And that is exactly what happens.

> *The sinful mind is hostile to God. It does not submit to God's law, nor can it do so.* (Romans 8:7)

The norms of the law of sin and death correspond exactly with the inner values of the flesh. Thus they reinforce each other. The flesh uses the force of law as an excuse: 'I couldn't help myself', and the law justifies the desires of the flesh: 'Everybody does it, so why can't you?'

Those under the law of sin and death end up *'gratifying the cravings of our sinful nature and following its desires and thoughts'* (Ephesians 2:3).

No wonder Paul, in the face of this seemingly impregnable system, cries, *'What a wretched man I am! Who will rescue me from this body of death?'* (Romans 7:24). We will see how deliverance comes.

Chapter 12

God's Answer for the Flesh

We now have to see God's answer to the problem created by the failure of humanity, a failure that has resulted in our bondage to the flesh and to the law of sin and death.

The old covenant failed to solve the problem, not because the law was deficient as law, but because it was external while the flesh was internal. Paul saw this very clearly:

> *For what the law was powerless to do in that it was weakened by the sinful nature, God did by sending his own Son...*　　　　　　　　　　　　(Romans 8:3)

External law on tablets of stone, even when written by the finger of God, could not win out against inner values diametrically opposed to the law.

The new covenant – internalized law

Therefore we find the prophets beginning to speak of a new covenant, radically different from the old covenant, and one which goes to the root of the problem in a totally different way:

> *'...I will make a new covenant with the house of Israel and with the house of Judah. It will not be like the covenant I made with their forefathers when I took them by the hand to lead them out of Egypt, because they broke my covenant, though I was a husband to them', declares the Lord.*

> *'This is the covenant that I will make with the house of Israel after that time', declares the Lord. 'I will put my law in their minds and write it on their hearts.*
> *I will be their God and they will be my people.'*
>
> (Jeremiah 31:31–33)

In other words, God says that the first step in a complete solution to the problem of covenant obedience is to internalize the law, to write it this time not on stone tablets but on human hearts. It is to become an internal law, not an external one.

New covenant values

Again God speaks through the prophet Ezekiel concerning the same new covenant:

> *'I will sprinkle clean water on you, and you will be clean; I will cleanse you from all your impurities and from all your idols. I will give you a new heart and put a new spirit in you; I will remove from you your heart of stone and give you a heart of flesh. And I will put my spirit in you and move you to follow my decrees and be careful to keep my laws.'*
>
> (Ezekiel 36:25–27)

Not only, then, is the law to be internalized, but something is to happen to the polluted human heart. Sin is to be cleansed from it and in it there is to be implanted a new set of inner values that will be in harmony with the internalized law. The problem of obedience is overcome! Obedience becomes the natural correspondence of inner values and inner law: in other words, spontaneous freedom.

Here are the two covenants contrasted:

Old covenant	*New covenant*
• Sin merely covered	• Sin cleansed away
• External law on stone tablets	• Internal law on tablets of human hearts
• Inner values of the flesh	• Inner values of the Spirit
• Heart of stone	• Heart of flesh

This is the new covenant under which we live today. It is explained with great clarity in 2 Corinthians 3. Paul begins there with the internalized law, verse 3, and leads on to the outcome in verse 17 which is liberty:

> *Where the Spirit of the Lord is, there is freedom.*

But we have to see in greater detail how, in fact, God accomplished this feat, so that we can enter into the living experience of our covenant rights.

The last Adam

The question we are faced with is, 'How, in real terms, is the law of God to be internalized? Can it actually be written on the heart?' I used to wonder at one time why Jesus took so long over our salvation, that is, why He spent over thirty years of human life before He went to the cross for us. Why could He not have come from heaven a perfect man, become our sin-bearer, died, risen from the dead and returned to the Father's right hand, all in a matter of days?

There are several reasons, of course, why it could not be that way, but I began to understand some of them when I read 1 Corinthians 15:45:

> *So it is written: 'The first man Adam became a living being', the last Adam, a life-giving spirit.'*

Jesus as the last Adam or, as somebody has said, 'Adam at last', a human being as he was meant to be, came to create a new beginning for humanity. He was the progenitor of new covenant people. Therefore He had to fulfill first of all in His own humanity the promises of the new covenant. His death was to solve the problem of human sin and His blood would cleanse the human heart from its filthiness and pollution. **But His life was the means by which the law of God was to be internalized.**

How did he do it? By obedience. By painstaking, persistent, perfect obedience, in every situation and in every circumstance, He wrote the law of God on His heart. In times of

stress, in times of boredom, against opposition and through-
out misunderstanding, over small issues and great, always
internalizing the law:

> *Therefore, when Christ came into the world, he said:*
> *'Sacrifice and offering you did not desire,*
> *   but a body prepared for me . . .*
> *Then I said, "Here I am – it is written about me*
> *   in the scroll –*
> *I have come to do your will, O God."'*
>
> (Hebrews 10:5, 7)

For the very first time in human history, a person lived in
such a relationship with God that He was able to say in all
honesty and in perfect truth, *'I always do the things that are
pleasing to him.'* Moreover, He had the Father's own testi-
mony to this fact: *'You are my Son, whom I love; with you I am
well pleased'* (Mark 1:11). In that one life the perfect law of
God was perfectly internalized.

In His human nature Jesus created two things that had
never existed before. We need to understand what they were.

Firstly He created a perfect human hatred for sin. God has
always perfectly hated sin. The unfallen angels perfectly hate
sin. But never before was there a human being who perfectly
hated sin. The very best Christian is unable to realize the true
nature of sin. Only the cross reveals what sin would do if left
unchecked – it would seek to kill God and wreck His universe.

This is an area of moral suffering and anguish in Jesus we
often overlook: living day by day in the presence of sin and
seeing what it was doing to human beings in His image.
Living among so much oppression and cruelty and evil,
among a suffering, perverted human race there grew in Jesus
an increasing hatred of sin. But at the cross when He, the
sinless man, experienced what it meant to become sin and
knew as a consequence the desolation of being shut out from
the Father's presence, there was irrevocably sealed in His
human heart a perfect and perfected hatred for sin.

The second thing that Jesus created that had never existed
before was a perfect human love for righteousness. The

unfallen angels perfectly love righteousness, but never before did a person love righteousness perfectly. In the human heart of Jesus, obedience brought a growing delight in the Father's will. But when He came to the cross and, accepting it as the Father's will, discovered that the outcome of that will and of His suffering obedience was the salvation of a world, there was sealed in the human heart of Jesus a perfect human love for righteousness and obedience.

But the last Adam was also to become a life-giving spirit, as we read in 1 Corinthians 15:45. What does this mean?

The human life of Jesus was a life that was completely open to the Holy Spirit. He was born of the Holy Spirit and baptized in the Holy Spirit. He healed the sick as a person anointed *'with the Holy Spirit and power'* (Acts 10:38), and He cast out demons by the Spirit of God. The miracles that Jesus did were miracles that an ordinary person, filled with the Holy Spirit, could perform. Everything that Jesus in His human nature knew of the Father and the Father's will, He knew by the revelation of the Holy Spirit.

There was a divine purpose in all this. Just as the satanic spirit worked in fallen humanity to produce the flesh, or the sinful nature, so **the Holy Spirit worked in the humanity of Jesus to create the set of inner values, that is, the 'new self', or 'the mind controlled by the Spirit'.**

You can see in Figure 13 the origins and relationships and authority of this new self.

The inner values of this new self are described in Galatians 5:22–23 as being *'love, joy, peace, patience, kindness, goodness, faithfulness, gentleness and self-control'.*

Against such things, Paul says, there is no law. Or to put it another way, 'The law of God is not against such things.' On the contrary, they are in perfect harmony and correspondence with the law.

The same new self is described in Ephesians 4:24 as *'created to be like God in true righteousness and holiness.'*

In the life of Jesus the result of this perfect harmony between inner values and the internalized law was perfect obedience. Out of this perfect obedience comes perfect freedom. In other words, Jesus was free to do spontaneously and

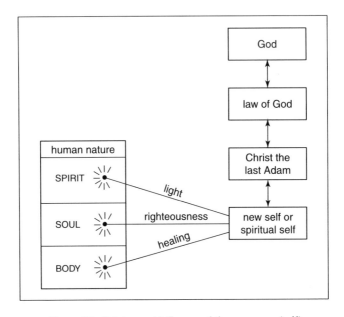

Figure 13: Origins and influence of the new man (**self**)

freely whatever He liked because the value system that guided His preferences or desires was in total harmony with the law of unselfish love. Jesus did not have to stop and ask Himself in every situation what the law of correct conduct was. It was in His heart so that He naturally, spontaneously and freely lived in harmony with it.

It is hard for us even to imagine what such a perfectly free human being would be like. Try to imagine someone with no complexes, no bondage, no inhibitions and no covert parts of his soul. Jesus was like that. You could not deceive Him; you could not manipulate Him; you could not coerce Him or condition Him.

People can always be controlled or manipulated by playing on two factors in human nature – greed and fear. Sometimes we call these tactics 'the carrot and the stick'. But there was no greed in Jesus. He coveted nothing for Himself. He said, *'...foxes have holes and the birds of the air have nests, but the Son of Man has nowhere to lay his head.'* And He was completely untroubled by the prospect. He had no fear. He slept through the storm, and constantly His word to His disciples was, 'Don't be afraid.' How do you get a hold on a person like that? Even Satan never managed it. At the very end Jesus was able to say, '... *the prince of this world is coming. He has no hold on me...*' (John 14:30).

Jesus was so free that He could even say of His life, '*No-one takes it from me, but I lay it down of my own accord. I have authority to lay it down and authority to take it up again*' (John 10:18). That, surely, is the ultimate freedom.

Chapter 13

Experiencing
New Covenant Freedom

I have already emphasized that God's answer to human need is always found in two complementary and indivisible works: the work of the cross, and the work of the Spirit. We shall see that the same holds true in the present case.

The work of the cross

Up to this point, all that Jesus had done in internalizing the law of God was, as it were, locked up in His individual humanity. There had to be a way for this to be transmitted to the whole race of new covenant people. The New Testament discloses how this was done.

In John 12:31–33 we read these words:

> 'Now is the time for judgement upon this world; now the prince of this world will be driven out. But I, when I am lifted up from the earth, will draw all men to myself.' He said this to show the kind of death he was going to die.

Usually we take this verse to mean that when we lift Jesus up – by preaching, or teaching, or testifying about Him, or by our lives expressing His grace – then He will attract people to Himself. That is true. A modern writer has expressed it beautifully: 'Jesus Christ is so holy and so attractive, that if we saw Him we would love Him even if He had never redeemed us.'

But that is not what Jesus is primarily referring to here. The context of the saying is His death and what is meant is this: when Jesus came to the cross, His individual personality became a corporate one. It incorporated all those who would believe in Him. Satan, the ruler of this world, is ejected from us and we are drawn into Him to become one with Him and part of Him.

In John chapter 13 we have the account of the incident in the upper room when Jesus began to wash the disciples' feet. In verse 8 we read:

> *'No', said Peter, 'you shall never wash my feet.'*
> *Jesus answered, 'Unless I wash you, you have no part in me.'*

The converse of this statement of Jesus then means, 'If I do wash you, you have part in me.' It is because we have part in Him, and thus, His humanity incorporated into us, that it is also true that when He died, we died; when He was buried, so were we; when He rose from the dead, we rose in Him.

> *Or don't you know that all of us who were baptized into Christ Jesus were baptized into his death? We were therefore buried with him through baptism into death in order that, just as Christ was raised from the dead through the glory of the Father, we too may live a new life.* (Romans 6:3–4)

We now have to see the effect that this incorporation into Christ has on our relationship with the flesh and our bondage to the law of sin and death.

> *For we know that our old self was crucified with him so that the body of sin might be done away with, that we should no longer be slaves to sin...* (Romans 6:6)

What does this mean? It means that the cross does away with (or makes of no effect) the line of authority that binds us to the law of sin and death. **We are free of the authority**

that has made us slaves to sin. The compelling and dominating effect of the inner values of the sinful nature is rendered powerless. Its hostility to the law of God, unchanged though that is, can no longer keep us in chains. We can, by a simple decision of our will, come free from the flesh, not because of our strength of will but because the cross, and our death there, has ended the power that it had over us.

The work of the Holy Spirit

In John chapter 7 we have the record of Jesus' visit to Jerusalem for the Feast of Tabernacles. Part of the ritual of the feast was the ceremony of pouring out, at the base of the altar, water from the pool of Siloam. While Jesus was watching this something stirred in His spirit and we read that He stood and cried out,

> *'If anyone is thirsty, let him come to me and drink. Whoever believes in me, as the Scripture has said, streams of living water will flow from within him.'* (John 7:37–38)

Then John goes on to explain that Jesus was speaking of the Holy Spirit whom those who believed in Him were to receive: *'Up to that time the Spirit had not been given, since Jesus had not yet been glorified.'*

Why was the Spirit not then yet given? He was waiting for something. He was waiting for Jesus to complete the perfected set of inner values we have been speaking about. To build into them every capacity and every resource that we would ever need in this life: perfect love, perfect faith, perfect obedience, perfect forgiveness.

He was waiting until Jesus came to the cross and His individual personality became a corporate one that incorporated us. He was waiting until the atonement was a finished work and the problem of our sin separating us from the Father was dealt with.

He was waiting until Jesus broke the ultimate barriers of death itself, and was, by the same Spirit, raised to resurrection life – death having no more dominion over Him. Then the Spirit was given.

> *. . . he breathed on them and said, 'Receive the Holy Spirit.'*
> (John 20:22)

The new self, the inner person, sometimes called just 'the spirit' came into the disciples at that point. When the Head of the Body entered into resurrection life, He breathed that resurrection life into the members of His body. A totally new set of inner values and an internalized law, written not on tablets of stone but on the heart, came into their life.

One nature or two?

I am aware that we are now in an area that has sometimes generated controversy; that is, the question as to whether a Christian has one nature or two. In other words, is there an 'old me' that wants to sin and a 'new me' that doesn't? If I sin, who is responsible – the old me or the new me? Who is the 'I' who yields to the old me? Am I really me when I am sinning or really me when I am righteous?

Personally, I do not believe that the Christian has two natures. I am me, and thus responsible for everything I do. I believe the facts can be better understood by seeing them as two competing authority systems, and two rival sets of inner values. The unregenerate self has only one authority system – the law of sin and death – and only one set of inner values – the flesh. The Christian alone has two options, as you can see from Figure 14.

Let me give you a personal experience that will illustrate what I mean. I used to be a very heavy smoker, and although I had many times tried to break the habit, I never succeeded beyond three days at a time. In short, it 'had me licked' and I knew it.

Nevertheless, the night I was baptized in the Holy Spirit, the Lord Jesus, as a kind of extra bonus thrown in (because I had much more important things on my mind that night than smoking), delivered me instantly and totally

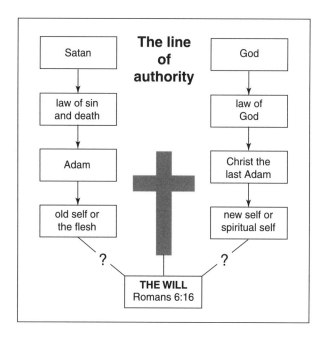

Figure 14: Liberation of the will

from all desire for tobacco. I had no withdrawal symptoms, I had no craving to smoke, I had no reaction at all. It was just as though I had never ever smoked in my life. It was wonderful, because nothing like that had ever happened to me before.

About three or four years later I went through a very severe personal crisis, when everything in my life seemed to collapse. Right in the middle of this traumatic upheaval, someone gave me a cigarette. I lit and smoked it, and then smoked a second one. Later, I noticed a curious thing. My head had not been swimming, nor had I felt as though my mouth was full of blotting paper. It was just as though I had never stopped smoking. I could quite easily have resumed my old 40-a-day habit. That is now about seventeen years ago; I have not smoked since, nor have I wanted to.

The point I want to make is this. There are not two Tom Marshalls, labeled like sections of a restaurant, 'Smoking' and

'Non-smoking'. There is only one Tom Marshall. But there is still in existence the full range of habits (smoking is only one of the less nasty of them) that made up my way of life. They are all primed up and ready to go. At any time, obedience to them can reactivate any or all of them. Sometimes my 'obedience' to them does just that. But I am not stuck with them. The glorious fact is that I need not be under the power of any of them, because the cross de-activates them and leaves me free. I can leave them to molder away and gather dust until I die, or until Jesus comes.

It is like having two alternative computer programs. (As they say: 'Garbage in – garbage out!') A program can only produce what has been put into it. The unregenerate person has only one program: the flesh. It can produce only what is in it: the works of the flesh that Paul describes in Galatians 5:19. The Christian has two programs: because of the cross he can unplug the old self – the flesh – and plug in the new self. That program can only produce what is in it, the fruit of the Spirit described in Galatians 5:22.

Here is how the programs compare:

The flesh (old self)	*The Spirit (new self)*
hostile against God	hostile against Satan
not subject to the law of God	not subject to the law of sin and death
produces:	produces:
darkness in the spirit	light in the spirit
sin in the soul	righteousness in the soul
sickness in the body	healing and health in the body
inner values:	inner values:
the works of the flesh	the fruit of the Spirit

The two programs are mutually exclusive. We cannot live with both plugged in simultaneously.

> *For the sinful nature desires what is contrary to the Spirit, and the Spirit what is contrary to the sinful nature. They are in conflict with each other . . .*   (Galatians 5:17)

By disconnecting the flesh and walking in the life of the spiritual self, we discover a glorious harmony between inner values and the internalized law, so that obedience to that law – the law of unselfish love – becomes not only possible but natural; and, because it is natural, it is freedom.

Walking in the Spirit

Many of the difficulties that we have experienced over entering into the reality of what we see in the cross have come from our neglect of the vital work of the Holy Spirit, always complementary to and indivisible from the work of the cross. In this particular context the work of the Spirit is two-fold:

1. His is the power that liberates our will from the bondage of habitual surrender to the demands of the flesh.
2. He is the one who educates us in living by the internalized law.

We must look briefly but carefully at each of these in turn. As human beings, made in the image of the Triune God, we are also a tri-unity: that is to say, we are spirit, soul and body (1 Thessalonians 5:23).

*   The **human spirit** is that part of a person that is regenerated; that is, it is the part which becomes the dwelling place within us of the Holy Spirit.
*   The **soul** (Greek *psyche*) is that part of human beings consisting of the mind, the will, the emotions or affections.

In unregenerate people, and in many Christians, the aim of the soul is to rule or dominate the person. But in God's order the spirit is the part of a person that is intended to rule his personality and be the integrating center of his being.

Walking in the Spirit means that the soul yields up its desire to rule, and submits to the authority of the human spirit, inhabited by the Holy Spirit.

God will never force the human will. This means that the power of the Holy Spirit within the human spirit will never be released into the area of the soul without the free response of the soul. As far as the will is concerned, the response that bridges the gap from soul to spirit is **obedience**. When we reach out in a response of obedience, the power of the Holy Spirit is released into the area of the will and breaks the yoke of bondage. It is the Holy Spirit in His anointing who breaks the yoke, who brings *'freedom for the captives and release from darkness for the prisoners'* (Isaiah 61:1). There is no habit, no compulsion, no bondage, no shackle on the will, that the Spirit of the Lord will not break to set us free.

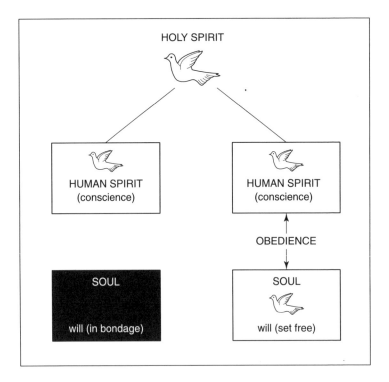

Figure 15: Obedience is the key

Then there is the educating work of the Holy Spirit. You may call it sanctification if you wish to be more theological, but again we must understand clearly what is meant.

The work of the Spirit is to apply the law of God to our lives in such a way that we are not trapped into legalism or self-conscious spirituality. We are meant to trust the reality of the work of God within us, so that we can live freely and spontaneously out of what we are, just so long as we respond to the educating work of the Spirit within us.

What does He do? He does what He did in Jesus: He writes the law on our heart. And the law sets us free!

Those of us with an evangelical background may find it hard to believe in the liberating power of the law. But the purpose of redemption was, as Paul says in Romans 8:4,

> *in order that the righteous requirements of the law might be fully met in us, who do not live according to the sinful nature but according to the Spirit.*

The law written on our hearts

The Holy Spirit will take us in hand, time and again, over our breaches of the law of unselfish love; if we respond He will write part of that law in our hearts. And let me tell you this: when He writes that law in our hearts, we become very tender in our conscience ever after on that point.

I remember one night, shortly after I had been baptized in the Holy Spirit, going with my wife to a little Assembly of God meeting near our home. Those dear saints were so noisy that somehow I couldn't get my thoughts together. I was very new to it all, and I spent the evening wishing they would just be quiet so I could at least think!

I went home quite out of sorts. I was in the bathroom washing my hands, when the Lord spoke to me. He said, 'You were critical tonight.' It was so unexpected that I didn't even have time to duck for cover! I replied, 'Yes, Lord, I was critical all right.' Then the Lord asked, 'And who were you criticizing?' I was suddenly smitten. 'Lord, I was criticizing You.'

It was true. There they were, the Lord and His people, enjoying each other immensely, and there I had been, full of carping, petulant criticism of them both. I had to get down on my knees right there on the bathroom floor and apologize to the Lord.

But that night the Holy Spirit wrote a law on my heart: a law that set me free from criticizing the way the saints of God worship. They can be as noisy or as quiet as they like. I am free to enjoy it either way. Not because I school myself not to criticize, but because there is a law on my heart concerning the question, and the internalized law sets me free.

We need to learn, consciously, to trust ourselves into the Spirit's hands for this. It is even harder perhaps to trust each other into the hands of the Holy Spirit to do it His way in His own time. We have the strange idea that we need to supervise the Holy Spirit to make sure He does a proper job.

Sometimes He may take us up over what seems a very small matter, and for a time let pass things that we – or others looking at us – consider far more important.

I remember one day at morning break going into the cafeteria at work. As I sat down one of my colleagues was in the middle of telling a story, and as he finished I remembered something that had happened to me. Well, I made my story a bit larger than real life. I embroidered it with one or two things that didn't actually happen exactly as I told them, but made the account more humorous. And suddenly I was so convicted that I had to leave my cup of tea and go and sort it out with the Lord.

Now, if I related this in some places, people would think, 'What a holy Joe! A little exaggeration and the Holy Spirit convicts him.' That isn't the point. There were, and are, far bigger issues in my life that the Lord hasn't faced me with. But that day He chose to write a law on my heart about telling lies. When we allow Him to take these gracious, divine initiatives and learn to respond to what He is doing in our lives, things get done, problems are solved, and something is perfected.

We, in fact, are ourselves changed, from one degree of glory to another, but always in the direction of liberty –

'where the Spirit of the Lord is, there is freedom' (2 Corinthians 3:17). There is liberty to live spontaneously and authentically from where we are, freely and naturally responding to the guidance of the internalized law, and discovering that obedience is meant to be not only possible but natural to the child of God.

PART IV

Chapter 14

Freedom to be Ourselves

One of the most puzzling questions facing the sincere Christian concerns the attitude that we are meant to adopt towards **ourselves**.

On the one hand, we are constantly warned against pride – the deadliest sin of all, and one that ruined the most exalted being God ever created. Most of us, if the truth be known, are more prone to self-pity, self-indulgence and self-protection, than really serious pride. But to avoid either danger, we are likely to adopt self-denial, self-abasement and self-effacement as Christian ideals, however far short of them we may fall in practice.

On the other hand, there are passages in the Bible that clearly hold up self-regard as the model upon which we should base our relationships with others: '... *love your neighbor as yourself'* (Matthew 19:19), for example; or *'husbands ought to love their wives as their own bodies'* (Ephesians 5:28).

Does that then mean that we are to deny, abase, or efface those others? Every Christian counselor has met people who really love their neighbors the way they love themselves – with disastrous results! To feel that we are inadequate, worthless, unwanted or unlovable can have a ruinous effect, not only on our own personality but also on our ability to form satisfying relationships with other people, and with God Himself. The deep hurts and damaged self-esteem that many people acquire in early childhood inhibit and sometimes maim the lives of even devout Christian men and women.

Yet, when all this has been said, we still must concede that there is an incurable self-centeredness about so much of our best and highest endeavors. The so-called 'healing ministry' or charismatic emphasis on Christian experience is not exempt from this. Attention can so easily become locked on to **my** need, **my** experience, **my** healing, **my** ministry, **my** gifts ... We can remain essentially self-centered or person-centered rather than God centered.

How then are we meant to live with the self? Because live with it we must. If we alternate, according to the preaching or teaching of the moment, between harsh, repressive measures and soft over-indulgence, we must not be surprised if we fail to achieve maturity. What we are most likely to produce, in fact, is the result brought about by parents who treat their child according to the whim of the moment – a child that has been 'spoiled'.

For most of my Christian life I lived with this generally muddled and contradictory attitude toward myself. Then a counseling experience some years ago led me to re-examine the whole subject in the light of what the Bible was really saying.

I had been speaking with a young married woman who had been going through a difficult time, which was compounded by feelings of self-doubt and general uncertainty about herself. She felt useless and hopeless, a problem to her prayer group, no help to her husband and children, and a sad disappointment to God, after some years of Christian experience. Regardless of the objective truth of the matter, that was exactly how she felt about herself, marooned in a vast, howling wilderness.

We talked for a while and then prayed together. While we were praying, the Lord gave me a word for her. Part of it surprised me so much that for a while I just could not believe that I had it right. The Lord was saying to that young woman that He really liked her! Now, I knew, of course, that the Lord **loves** us. But that He could also **like** us – that I had never really contemplated. What? Like us? Take pleasure in our company? Admire our taste? Enjoy our personality or temperament? Even take a delight in the way we look? That was something new.

It took time, but when I was ale to put aside my preconceptions and the bias that were really an expression of my own needs in this area, I began to clearly hear what the Bible had been saying all along. What is more, I began to glimpse areas of freedom and healing that were truly exciting.

Since then, I have begun to live in at least enough of it to know that it is not a mirage but a genuine part of our inheritance. It is, in fact, part of the glorious freedom that belongs to every child of God.

But to find our way into it, we have to go right back to the very beginnings of our history.

The created self

The early chapters of Genesis are foundational in many areas of truth, but in none more so than for understanding the true nature and essential being of humanity. Two statements concerning the person God created are particularly important.

▶   **First, the Bible declares that people were made to be loving beings.**

In Genesis 1:26 we read that God said, *'Let us make man in our image, in our likeness'.* What are we to make of this? The idea of human beings in God's image has been interpreted in various ways, but I believe it can be understood as follows.

In the material creation, God has manifested His power and wisdom for all to see.

> *For since the creation of the world God's invisible qualities – his eternal power and divine nature – have been clearly seen, being understood from what has been made . . .*
> (Romans 1:20)

But because He is Father, God purposed something even more wonderful. He purposed to extend His own love-nature to the created universe, by creating a man in His image and after His likeness. In other words, people were made to mirror-image in Himself the inner dynamic of the Godhead, and that inner dynamic has been revealed to us as love (1 John 4:8). So we were made with love at the heart of our beings; we were made loving beings.

Because of this, we find that Adam, even at the level of his creaturely humanness, was incomplete without someone like himself to love. God said, *'It is not good for the man to be alone. I will make a helper suitable for him'* (Genesis 2:18). Therefore Eve was created, flesh of his flesh, bone of his bone, so that together in the union of love they might be Adam – mankind.

One of the hardest things for us to understand about human beings as they are today – once we know the original ground-plan of our nature – is cruelty. In our generation we have seen so much of it that we are becoming hardened, and thus liable to overlook the extreme pervasiveness of cruelty. It lies behind almost every form of human sin. Sometimes it is open, sometimes it is hidden. Sometimes it is physical, sometimes psychological. It is the driving force behind a rampant social evil like pornography. For pornography, there has to be a victim. Therefore, 'no victim – no pornography.'

Nevertheless, every time we see or experience cruelty, it is still something of a shock, because intuitively we know that people were not meant to be like that. We do not call cruelty 'humanity'; we call it 'inhumanity'. Human beings, we know full well, were made to love. We are properly human only when we are at least trying to be true to ourselves in this regard.

▶ **Secondly, Genesis makes it clear that human beings were created as selves or egos.**

In Genesis 2:7 we read,

> *the Lord God formed the man from the dust of the ground and breathed into his nostrils the breath of life, and the man became a living being.*

In other words, human beings have an ego or a self because we were created that way. It is the way God intended us to be. It is important that we give this fact its full weight, because it necessarily follows that if God made the self, He is not going to blot it out or eliminate it. He may have to redeem it and renew it, but He is not going to destroy it.

Yet often our preaching and teaching conveys, at least by inference (and sometimes explicitly), that destroying the self is God's aim. In sanctification, so the message goes, the Holy Spirit aims to blot out the human self and replace it with Christ. Although the person may walk about and go through the motions of living, ideally the self has disappeared and Christ has taken over. If this is so, the truly sanctified Christian sounds oddly like a kind of spiritual zombie, from whom all individuality and identity have been erased, so that only Christ appears.

Even when I didn't know what was wrong with this kind of teaching, I somehow sensed that it didn't fit the facts. It puzzled me that what was conveyed by the preaching appeared to produce quite opposite results in practice. For example, the most spiritual Christians I knew were also the most authentic individuals. They were unmistakably real people. The only sameness about them was that they were so different from one another! I now understand that this individuality is, in fact, God-ordained. The Creator has gone to most extraordinary lengths to make each one of us a 'one-off' production, never to be exactly duplicated ever again.

I am now frankly suspicious of any form of training, teaching or method of worship that seeks to force people into a common mold. God is not turning out spiritual Christians in batches of ten, all thinking alike, praying alike, believing alike, worshiping alike. That is a human method of mass production, not God's creativity at work. God's purpose, I learn from the New Testament, is to fill the universe with infinite variety, what Paul calls *'the manifold wisdom of God'*, or in Berkeley's translation, *'the many-sided wisdom of God'* (Ephesians 3:10). For this glorious harmony God needs our individuality to be fully expressed, yet held in harmony with each other's individuality.

The purpose of creation

One of the fundamental revelations of the Bible is that from all eternity, the Triune God has existed in a relationship between the Father, the Son, and the Spirit, that perfectly expresses the infinite fullness of divine being. John, in particular, strains to express this within the limitations of human language. He uses three very rich words that together convey, in a kind of stereoscopic effect, something of the amazing richness of God's being. All three can be found in John chapter 17.

▶ The first is **life**.

 Now this is eternal life: that they may know you, the only true God, and Jesus Christ, whom you have sent.   (John 17:3)

▶ The second is **glory**.

 And now, Father, glorify me in your presence with the glory I had with you before the world began.   (John 17:5)

▶ The third is **love**.

 Father, I want those you have given me to be with me where I am, and to see my glory, the glory you have given me because you loved me before the creation of the world.

(John 17:24)

Human beings created in the image of God were not only to mirror this dynamic within Himself: they were to **become partakers** of the life and the love and the glory of the Godhead. This was in God's heart from the beginning.

 ... He chose us in him before the creation of the world ... In love he predestined us to be adopted as his sons through Jesus Christ, in accordance with his pleasure and will – to the praise of his glorious grace ...   (Ephesians 1:4–6)

This was the real glory with which human beings were crowned in their creation. *'You made him a little lower than the heavenly beings and crowned him with glory and honor'* (Psalm 8:5).

But how was humanity to come to share this glory? The answer is that in the core of the human soul, God had placed the great dynamic of **love**. This love was meant to be poured out to God, so that in turn God could share his love and life and glory with us.

One of the most wonderful discoveries I have made about God is that somehow everything He does and everything He commands always ends up being for our benefit. Often we think God's commands are in order to extract something from us, but they are always in order to **give**.

> *And now, O Israel, what does the LORD your God ask of you but to fear the LORD your God, to walk in all his ways, to love him, to serve the LORD your God with all your heart and with all your soul, and to observe the LORD's commands and decrees that I am giving you today for your own good?*
> (Deuteronomy 10:12–13)

God's commands are for our good. When He commands us to love Him, it is for our benefit, not His. It is not that God needs our love; it is we who need both to love Him and be loved by Him. Our whole health and happiness depends on us satisfying our need for love. If we do not succeed in doing so, we will without fail suffer spiritually, mentally, emotionally and physically.

The self as a goal-directed mechanism

God's purpose in creation was to share His love-nature with us. That has always been the Father's declared intention.

> *For those God foreknew he also predestined to be conformed to the likeness of his Son, that he might be the firstborn among many brothers.* (Romans 8:29)

How was this to be accomplished? The answer is that in the constitution of human nature, God created the capability for this to be done. He created the self. The self is a goal-directed mechanism. It reproduces in human nature whatever it is focused on. It was made that way; there is no other way it can function. Whatever it is locked on to, it reproduces in us. It works consciously and unconsciously, waking or sleeping, to produce in us the replica of what it is occupied with. In Adam God meant the self, directed towards the tree of life, to produce the likeness of Christ in created human beings. In other words, the Word was to become flesh in Adam and Eve.

Chapter 15

The Fallen Self

What actually happened in the garden?

Already we can sense that something drastic has happened to humanity. Something has caused the deep and powerful drives within our nature to function destructively, although originally they were put there for creative purposes. Human nature seems like a machine that has toppled off its stand, but with the motor still running, wheels spinning, pistons pumping, levers flailing. It gets nowhere, accomplishes nothing, and is a danger to itself and everything around it. We must go back to Genesis chapter 3 to see what actually happened to human beings made in the image and likeness of God.

In the biblical record of the Fall, we find an amazing thing. Satan, the most self-centered being in the universe, comes to Eve and accuses God of being selfish. 'God', he says, 'wants all He can get from you. But will He share with you the tree of the knowledge of good and evil? Not likely.' *'For God knows that when you eat of it your eyes will be opened, and you will be like God, knowing good and evil'* (Genesis 3:5).

The alluring possibility put before Eve amounted to this: why waste your love on God who does not appreciate it? Reach out for the forbidden fruit, and **you can be your own god**. Then that great resource of love within your nature can be all for yourself.

We greatly misunderstand the basic problem of humanity if we think that the first sin was only disobedience, as we have generally been taught. The sin was first **injustice**, not disobedience, although disobedience came into it. You see, they took something concerning which God had said, 'This is mine. All the other trees in the garden are yours, but this is mine alone.'

Human beings would not accept that there was something they could not have for themselves. They stepped unjustly across the line God had drawn. They transgressed; they took something that did not belong to them, in order to satisfy their own selves or egos. The same thing is seen in small children. The hardest lesson a child has to learn is not obedience but justice. 'You cannot keep that; it does not belong to you', or 'You cannot have all the sweets for yourself; some of them are for the other children.'

The fruit of the tree of the knowledge of good and evil offered such wonderful possibilities: food, pleasure, and wisdom. These correspond to real and God-created needs within human beings: the need for life, the need for love, and the need for wisdom. The deception lay in the fact that these things never were in the tree of the knowledge of good and evil. They were only available from the tree of life, that is Christ, and from no other source.

> *In him was life, and that life was the light of men.*
> (John 1:4)

> *... live a life of love, just as Christ loved us ...*
> (Ephesians 5:2)

> *... Christ, in whom are hidden all the treasures of wisdom and knowledge.* (Colossians 2:2–3)

But to eat of the tree of life meant that Adam and Eve must love God with all their heart and all their soul and all their mind and all their strength. It was at this point of choice – love given to God or love invested in themselves – that they were tested, and failed.

The effects of the Fall

The Fall radically affected both the inner constitution of human nature and, in consequence of that, all our external relationships also. You can see this expressed in Figure 16.

First, there occurred a deep investment of love on the human self or ego. From being a self, human beings became selfish. From being an ego, we became egocentric.

This is already apparent in Genesis 3:6. The fruit was good for food (for Eve); it was a delight to (her) eyes, it was desirable to make (her) wise. God never enters into consideration at all.

Secondly, as a direct consequence of sin, human beings lost their fellowship and their relationship with God. They fell into a state of death, cut off from access to the tree of life.

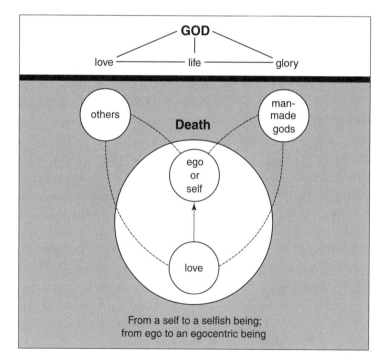

Figure 16: From a self to a selfish being

*And the L*ORD *God said, 'The man has now become like one of us, knowing good and evil. He must not be allowed to reach out his hand and take also from the tree of life and eat, and live forever. So the* LORD *God banished him from the Garden of Eden to work the ground from which he had been taken. After he drove the man out, he placed on the east side of the Garden of Eden cherubim and a flaming sword flashing back and forth to guard the way to the tree of life.*
(Genesis 3:22–24)

This expulsion was the mercy of God. For God now to share His life and glory with people who now were so fixated in self-love, would have inflated the human ego to demonic proportions. Human beings would have become devils incarnate, beyond the possibility of redemption.

So, human beings were sent out from the garden until the problem of their sin could be solved. Their future access to the tree of life could now only be secured by the way of another tree, the tree of Calvary.

Thirdly, human beings, cut off from living fellowship with God, are also cut off from obtaining true knowledge of Him. They fall back on the worship of their own degenerate concepts of God.

. . . their thinking became futile and their foolish hearts were darkened. Although they claimed to be wise, they became fools and exchanged the glory of the immortal God for images made to look like mortal man and birds and animals and reptiles.   (Romans 1:21–23)

Human beings made in the image of God now make gods in the image of human beings. In other words, they worship the projections of their own egos. Human history is littered with the terrible gods that people have created: cruel, promiscuous, disfigured and perverted, created out of the depths of the broken, disordered human soul. Worse, focused on these distorted gods, people increasingly reproduce the same distortion in themselves. They *'followed worthless idols and became worthless themselves'* (Jeremiah 2:5). What else can the self do?

Fourthly, not only are human beings in their self-centered state unable to love God, they have lost the capacity to love others in a truly disinterested, altruistic way. We love other people merely so that they will love us and meet our need for love. If love is not reciprocated we feel cheated, spurned and rejected. Sooner or later we 'break off' such one-way relationships in order to look for another where there will be some return on our investment of ourselves.

This ultimate self-seeking behavior is recognized by all perceptive observers of human nature. C.S. Lewis speaks in one of his books about those who 'spend their lives for others'. You can always tell the 'others', he says, by their hunted look! A secular psychiatrist wrote recently, 'When a young man says to a young woman, "I love you," what he is really saying is "I want you; I love me."'!' Another writer says that every human love relationship is really the expression of three desires: 'Let me do what I like. Give me what I want. Prove to me that I am somebody.'

Fifthly, the self as a goal-directed mechanism is cut off from its true goal, that is, from the tree of life. It still functions the only way in which it can – it seeks a goal and reproduces that object in its nature. What goal is now available to the self? It is only the impressions, feelings and responses that we experience in relation to other people. **This is the origin of the self-image**, the concept of ourselves that we acquire first as small children and add to all our lives. It is built up from many sources: the way our parents treat us, whether as children we felt loved and valued, or neither; the success or failure we experience in school, with friendships and so on; even our body image.

But because we are now focused on flawed, distorted people in a flawed, distorted world, our self-image is also flawed. It is not the accurate truth about ourselves. It reflects the problems of our parents and friends as much as it reflects us, but it is the only image we have of ourselves to go on. The power of the self-image is that we tend to live it out very faithfully and we work very hard to make it true about ourselves. Therefore, if our self-image is a negative one, if we feel a failure and think we are worthless, the self works very hard to produce someone who fails and proves to be quite worthless.

Finally, the self-centered universe into which people have now locked themselves becomes a fertile source of fear, anxiety and depression. Anything that appears to endanger or threaten the self induces fear and anxiety, anger or hurt. Why? *'For where your treasure is, there your heart will be also'* (Luke 12:34).

Similarly, we find it hard to accept failure. We are demanding, quite unconsciously, divine standards of perfection from ourselves. When we fail, we are prone to depression, gloom and – in extreme cases – total withdrawal.

What about the Christian?

We need to state quite clearly that for many, probably nearly all Christians, conversion (or the new birth) does not of itself solve the problem of a very deep fixation of love on the self. This is a matter of such common experience that we hardly need proof; but we need to see why it is so, in order to find the answer.

The unregenerate person can first become aware of his need when the Holy Spirit brings conviction to his conscience. Conscience is that function of the human spirit that judges our behavior; but conscience is very much more sensitive to wrong acts than wrong motives. Before conversion, conscience causes us to experience guilt over the sins we have committed, and when we repent and turn in faith to Christ for the first time, it is forgiveness for these things that we experience.

The real problem, however, is the very deep love investment on the self that takes place in levels below the conscious mind. This principally affects our **motivation**. In other words, we often do things that are right in themselves, but we do them for wrong, self-seeking reasons. Our conscience is not at first very sensitive to this fact. The human mind has, furthermore, a whole battery of unconscious, psychological defense mechanisms that operate to prevent the conscience from detecting the problem, and subjecting us to painful self-insights.

Let us look at some of this ego-armor that we have developed.

Rationalization is one form. That is, inventing plausible but spurious reasons for something we have already decided to do anyway. Pilate, washing his hands and protesting his innocence of the blood of Jesus, was rationalizing his position. The truth was that he was giving way to cowardice: *'If you let this man go, you are no friend of Caesar's'* (John 19:12).

Projection is another defense mechanism. We see clearly in other people the very problems we have in ourselves but cannot face up to. The person with a critical spirit is likely to be always complaining about others criticizing; the loveless person sees nothing but lack of love in others; and so on. This is the main thrust of the parable about the splinter and the beam. The person with the log in his eye mysteriously considers himself to be an expert at discerning splinters in the eyes of others!

Repression is a third – and the most dangerous – way. Unpleasant insights that we dare not face up to are buried so deep that we have genuinely forgotten that they are there at all.

> *'For this people's heart has become callused; they hardly hear with their ears, and they have closed their eyes. Otherwise they might see with their eyes, hear with their ears, understand with their hearts and turn, and I would heal them.'*
> (Matthew 13:15)

What is repressed or buried is, however, still alive and active. Forgotten by the unconscious mind, it still discharges its bitterness into the streams of life.

God, however, is deeply concerned not only with our deeds but with our motivation. It is the pure in heart who will see God. The righteousness of the Kingdom that must exceed the righteousness of the scribes and Pharisees is a righteousness of intention and motivation. Therefore, the common experience of Christians is that **after** we are regenerate, **after** we have genuinely become children of God, the Holy Spirit begins to probe into the depths of our personality to deal with the hidden streams of motivation. Thereupon we become aware of something more than sins. We become aware of a selfish principle that seems to poison the entire depths of our being. Listen to the anguished cry of Paul's heart in Romans chapter 7.

> ... *nothing good lives in me* ... *When I want to do good, evil is right there with me* ... *I see another law at work in the members of my body, waging war against the law of my mind and making me a prisoner of the law of sin* ... *What a wretched man I am! Who will rescue me from this body of death?*   (vv. 18, 21, 23, 24)

There is an answer. Yes, praise God, there is an answer! But first we must allow the Holy Spirit to reveal our need. He alone can penetrate the ego defenses, because He has access to all levels of the mind, unconscious as well as conscious. In fact, it is precisely because the root of the problem is so deep within the personality that it is largely beyond the power of the conscious mind to do anything about it.

That is why it is fruitless for preachers to exhort their congregations to be more unselfish, if they don't go on to show how it can be done. Heavy pressure from the pulpit may make people feel guilty and cause them to try and be unselfish. They may even perform acts that are apparently unselfish. But it still leaves unresolved the question of why they chose so to act. Out of true, unselfish altruism or to escape from feelings of guilt? From selfless love, or in order to conform to the accepted concept of a Christian? Many **motives** for unselfish acts may themselves be fundamentally selfish.

This discovery lays the earnest Christian open to paralyzing self-doubt regarding the purity of his motives. Am I really serving Christ for His sake or just for selfish, 'safety' motives? Do I really love God or am I just saying I love Him so that He will be gracious to me? We can go through agonies of self-examination and recrimination. Let me tell you something wonderful. God wants us to be sure about our motivation, to know when we honestly desire to please Him and to know when self-seeking creeps in. Read on and find the means of this liberation as well.

Chapter 16

The Liberation of the Self

We have begun to see how deep and binding is the self-centeredness brought about by the Fall, and how it is reinforced in every generation by selfish choices that are continually being made. Clearly the answer to the problem – if there is an answer – must be equally radical. It turns out to be a devastating solution.

> *'If anyone would come after me, he must deny himself and take up his cross and follow me. For whoever wants to save his life will lose it, but whoever loses his life for me will find it.'* (Matthew 16:24–25)

Jesus says unequivocally that the answer to self-centeredness or selfishness is a cross.

The cross – threat or salvation?

When I was younger, we used to call a message on the cross as applied to the Christian life 'a challenging address'. That meant that it was very uncomfortable to listen to and you forgot it as quickly as possible afterwards! Somehow we find the cross a very threatening subject. The cross for Jesus? Yes, that is wonderful and we are so grateful that He went through it. But a cross for us? That is something quite different!

Peter clearly had a strong reaction to the cross when Jesus, as related in Matthew chapter 16, began to show His disciples that His purpose in going up to Jerusalem was to be crucified. He took the Lord aside and began to rebuke Him. I think Peter may have figured it out like this: 'If they crucify the Master, that's bad. Then they will probably crucify his disciples – and that's me!'

There is something about the cross that endangers something within us. But **what does the cross threaten?** The self – or self-love? This is a very crucial point to grasp.

It is not the self as self that is the problem: it is selfishness.

It is not that we have a self: it is that we now relate to the self in a totally wrong way.

From being a **means** for us to express love, the self has become the **goal** or **object** of love.

It is this fixation of love on the self as an end or object that has to be dealt with, in order that we can be free to love the self the way it was meant to be loved, as a means to an end. And that end is to love the Lord our God with all our heart and all our soul and all our mind and all our strength, and to love our neighbor as ourselves.

But Jesus also makes it plain that only something as drastic as a cross can break that deep fixation of love of the self. The language that Jesus uses is very strong: 'deny' means literally 'to utterly disown'.

To understand the principle at stake, turn to the story of Abraham in Genesis chapter 22. Remember how God gave Abraham a son in his old age: Isaac, the child of promise. Then one day God told Abraham,

> *'Take your son, your only son, Isaac, whom you love, and go to the region of Moriah. Sacrifice him there as a burnt offering on one of the mountains I will tell you about.'*
> (Genesis 22:2)

What was God doing? Isaac, you see, was not the promised seed. He was the means through whom the seed was to come, as Paul tells us in Galatians chapter 3, because the seed is Christ. In other words, Isaac was a means, not an end. God was dealing with Abraham as a man of faith. He had to save Abraham from doting on Isaac as the end, instead of a means to the end that God had in view. How Abraham struggled with the problem we are told in Hebrews chapter 11. Abraham had it worked out that he was going to have to kill Isaac, and cremate his body. But because the covenant promise was to come through Isaac, God would have to raise him from the ashes.

We know what actually happened. When the point was reached in Abraham's heart that he raised the knife to slay Isaac, the potential entanglement of his affections was broken. He was free. He received Isaac back 'from the dead', and enjoyed his presence until the day of his own death.

This is God's purpose in us also – to liberate us from the fixation of love on the self as a goal or end, so that we can, without danger, love ourselves freely as a means through which God's goal can be accomplished.

What cross?

The question then arises: what cross can deal with radical selfishness in my life in order to set me free? If you talk to some people about the cross in their lives they are likely to say, 'Wait half and hour and I'll introduce you; he'll be home from work soon.' Their cross is a person who frustrates or irritates them. For others, the cross is an uncongenial occupation that they are putting up with, hoping that somehow it will make them more sanctified. Some people regard sickness as a cross, or bereavement, or lack of money, or trying circumstances.

If you are hoping that one of these crosses will free you from self, or make you less self-centered, I am sorry. None of them will – not one of them. Trouble and sickness may, in fact, make us even more self-centered than before, contrary to what we may have been led to believe.

Take, for example, Psalm 102 which is the prayer of an afflicted man for mercy. In the first eleven verses he uses the personal pronoun, I, me or my, no fewer than twenty-eight times, two-and-a-half times for each verse. Where is the center of his attention? On himself. Contrast this with the beginning of Psalm 103, which is a psalm of praise for

God's mercies: *'Praise the* LORD, *O my soul ... praise his holy name ... forget not all his benefits'.*

We cannot crucify ourselves. We cannot put ourselves on the cross. Some try so strenuously to crucify themselves that they end up by almost spoiling themselves for the ordinary business of living. Furthermore, if we did manage to crucify ourselves, the result would be even more disastrous, because we would then build a shrine to our martyred self and worship there all the rest of our lives! Parents sometimes do that. They sacrifice themselves for their children's future, and then destroy the entire family relationship by continually reminding their children of what they gave up for them.

▶ **There is only one cross that can set us free from ourselves, and in doing so set the self free to be itself, and that is the cross of Jesus.**

In the Garden

The problem of human selfishness began in a garden – the Garden of Eden. The answer was found in another garden – the Garden of Gethsemane.

I often used to wonder at some of the strange aspects of the experience Jesus had when He came to Gethsemane. He was so troubled and distressed that He nearly died. The literal translation from the Greek in the gospel of Mark is that He was *'greatly astonished and distressed'*. I used to wonder what astonished Jesus in the Garden of Gethsemane. Not the cross, surely – He had always known about that. Often He had tried to speak to the disciples about it. All His life had been moving towards that hour, the hour of His lifting up, the time of His going to the Father.

Then there was that strange prayer: *'Not what I will, but what you want'*, prayed not once or twice but three times, in such mental and moral agony that His sweat was like drops of blood. What was the struggle? Always up to this point Jesus had been supremely confident of His ability to do the Father's will: *'I always do what pleases the Father.'* But now at the last there was a great, unexpected struggle to yield to the Father's will.

It is true that we are here in the realm of eternal things that will remain forever beyond our ability to entirely grasp. But I believe there is something so vital that we need to try to understand it, so fundamental to the whole of our experience that it will well repay the effort to get hold of it. Let us go back a little.

We have already referred to the revelation that in the incarnation, when the Word became flesh, the man Jesus began to live in a relationship with the Father and the Holy Spirit in which He experienced the life and love and glory of God. We have seen that everything that Jesus did in His humanity He did as a man filled with the Holy Spirit. Everything He knew of God He knew by the revelation of the Spirit. He did this, not to show us something but to share something with us. Therefore when He came to the cross, His individual humanity became a corporate humanity. It incorporated all who would believe in Him. He said, *'But I, when I am lifted up from the earth, will draw all men to myself'* (John 12:32).

Remember the inference from Jesus' statement in John 13:8: 'If I do wash you, you have **part in me**.' It is because of our incorporation in Him that His death becomes ours. We share His resurrection and we participate in His power.

But this incorporation has significance also for Jesus. In becoming our redeemer, Jesus, on the cross, took upon Himself more than just the guilt of our sin. He took upon Himself our sinfulness.

> *God made him who had no sin to be sin for us, so that in him we might become the righteousness of God.*
> (2 Corinthians 5:21)

In the Garden of Eden, human beings ate of the tree of the knowledge of good and evil and lost access to the tree of life. In the Garden of Gethsemane, the sinless Son of God and Son of Man experienced the fruit of that deadly tree, in order to give us access once again to the tree of life.

What do we mean by that? Not that Jesus sinned. No. But in the garden Jesus became experientially aware in Himself of the radical selfishness of the human nature He had come to set free. This is what amazed Him. He was astonished, and distressed to discover how deep and binding was the rebellious self-centeredness within the humanity He had come to redeem. That selfishness ran through human nature from top to bottom, infecting everything. It is born in injustice, fostered by generations of slavish obedience, iron-hard and intractable.

▶ **It was the radical selfish will of rebellious humanity that Jesus wrestled with in the Garden of Gethsemane. It was that will He bent to submit to the will of God.**

It was a struggle beyond comprehension. All we know is that it took agony and bloody sweat, and the ministry of an angel to strengthen Him, before it was done. But He did it. Praise His name! In Himself, for us, He did it! He broke the deep, self-centered fixation within human nature and, making it at last choose the Father's will, broke us free from radical selfishness.

Jesus knew very clearly that somehow He had to get through the cross as a human being. On the side of His divine nature He was untouchable and unchangeable. If on Calvary His humanity had broken, nothing in God would have altered. Nothing in God **could** alter. The eternal *Logos* would have gone back to heaven to the right hand of the Father, but we would have been eternally lost beyond redemption. Jesus had to get through Calvary as a human being, in order to get us through. When He came from His struggle in the garden and saw the disciples asleep, that must have been the point of His worst temptation. I believe that there Satan said to Him, 'You'll never make it. You are made of that same humanity as them and look, they couldn't even stay awake for You.' But, bless God! Jesus got through – as a human being – and therefore we are through. Because He lives, we live also.

The work of the cross and the work of the Spirit

We have come repeatedly to this point of realizing that the answer of God to all the problems of human nature lie in two inseparable divine operations: the work of the cross, and the work of the Holy Spirit. Let us see how this glorious provision meets us in our present need.

The work of the cross

The cross has made a way for the fixation of human love on the ego to be broken. The power and authority of this fixation ends at the cross.

> *I have been crucified with Christ and I no longer live, but Christ lives in me. The life I live in the body, I live by faith in the Son of God, who loved me and gave himself for me.*
> (Galatians 2:20)

When, on the ground of Calvary, we disown the right of the self to rule us, we can become free of its binding power. Thus the self must come to the cross, not to be destroyed, but to give up its illegitimate claim to rule.

How, therefore, do we apply the cross to this situation?

1. There has to be an act of **renunciation**, in which we utterly disown the self as the goal of our affections and the ruling center of our life. We, who gave it the place of dominion, must be the ones to dethrone it. Be very clear about this. Without the work of Christ on the cross, there is no way in which we could overcome the ego armor (selfishness) and come out from under its deceptive, insidious power. But without the consent of our will, the victory of Calvary will still remain inoperative as far as we are concerned.

2. There has to be an act of **recognition**, in which we appropriate the work of Calvary to accomplish this deliverance and to deal with the radical selfishness within our nature.

This may be a new dimension of the work of the cross for you. Let us go from what we already know as a bridge to what we do not yet know. When you came to the cross with your sin and your guilt, you realized your ultimate helplessness to do anything about it. But you also realized that on the cross, Jesus had, in fact, already dealt with both your guilt and your sin. So you yielded them up, and in simple trust accepted His forgiveness and His cleansing. What have you now discovered? Just that it works! The cross gives me a clean conscience. I am free from condemnation, and the enslaving power of sin has been broken in my life.

Understand that the cross deals with the root of sin, which is radical selfishness, in exactly the same way. I cannot break free from self-centeredness. The cross breaks me free. I accept that freedom just the same way that I accepted freedom from sin and guilt.

The work of the Holy Spirit

The work of the Holy Spirit is also two-fold:

1. **He enables us to make Jesus Lord.** He is the only one who can, for it is His central ministry to glorify Jesus and to reveal the essential lordship that belongs to His nature. The throne of my heart cannot remain empty. It was made to be filled. Through the Holy Spirit I discover that it was made to be occupied by the Lord Jesus Christ.

2. **He pours out the love of God within our hearts.** We come into the flow of the love-life-glory relationship with the Godhead, for which we were created. Love for God and the love of God floods through the self, out to God, and out to others. Now we can love out of fullness, not out of need. Now we need others to love in order to **release** the love of God that is in our heart, not to obtain the love we need.

In the testimonies of those who come to this place of self-surrender, it is deeply impressive to read what inevitably and invariably follows – an outpouring of divine love. This love is a burning reality sometimes overwhelming in its magnitude, love not merely believed in with the head but experienced with the entire being.

It seems that God is not content merely to take **our** love on faith. Constantly we are commanded to love Him with all our heart and all our soul and all our mind and all our strength. Why? It is because God wants to experience it. In the same way I am convinced that God does not intend us merely to take **His** love on faith. He wants us to experience it with every part of our being.

Why, then, do we not experience it more often? There may be various reasons, but the most common one is that the self is still in the way, seeking to be the object, seeking to have and to hold it for itself. God, in His mercy and concern for us will not allow it. Displace self from the throne room to the servants' quarters where it belongs, and it will become what it is ideally fitted to be: a channel for divine love to flow through, in an unending stream. Because the motivation of our heart is now pure, the lordship of Jesus becomes a reality in our lives. The 'on again, off again' lordship that existed before was really no lordship at all, because regardless of conscious intention, self was still on the throne.

Chapter 17

The Liberated Self

Now, at last, we can discover that not only are we set free from self, but self has also been set free. The purpose in dethroning self is not to discard it, but to fulfill it. Having 'lost' our self-life, we now find it. Wrongly situated in our life, self was always doomed to fear and frustration, struggling with a task for which it was totally unfitted and which was quite beyond it. Rightly related, however, the self has a glorious fulfillment ahead.

But – and this must be stressed – **there is no way to avoid the cross**. If we try to relate in positive, supportive, self-regarding ways towards a still-enthroned self-life, we are heading for disaster. Much that is good and true is being written and taught today about positive attitudes towards the self. They are things that need to be said. If they hope to produce sanctification apart from the cross, however, they are doomed to fail. Once the cross has done its work, and the self has been set free to be a means and not an end, real freedom becomes possible.

Freedom from insecurity

Every human being has the need to belong, the need for significance, and the need for reasonable security.

If you turn back to Figure 16, you will see that the self-centered life has an in-built, basic insecurity. There can be no sense of belonging because the life is locked in on itself. There

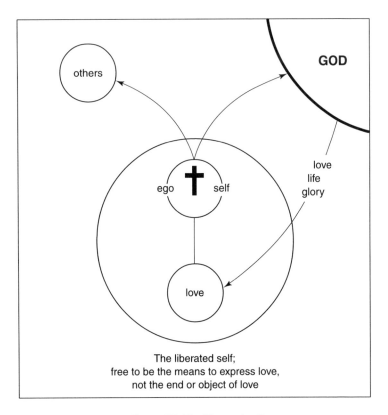

The liberated self;
free to be the means to express love,
not the end or object of love

Figure 17: The liberated self

is a lack of significance because the ego is the entire center of its little universe. There is no security because so many external experiences are interpreted as threats to the ego, due to the massive and inordinate investment of love in it. But when the self is set free to be a channel for love, as in Figure 17, there comes into being the possibility of genuine and meaningful relationships, firstly with God and then with other people.

Someone described a friend of mine in this way: 'He always seems to have such a secure relationship with God.' The self in its proper role, fulfilling its proper function, opens up the way for this to be the experience of every child of God.

The Amplified Version of the Bible puts it this way:

For he, God himself, has said, I will not in any way fail you, nor give you up, nor leave you without support. I will not, I will not, I will not in any degree leave you helpless, nor forsake you, nor let you down, nor relax my hold on you. Assuredly not!   .   (Hebrews 13:5)

The self now acquires genuine significance. So often there is the feeling within us that what we have to offer God or others is of little value, and is unlikely to be appreciated. Therefore we either do not offer it or we offer it without expecting or being open to a response.

But we now discover that we are significant to God. We are 'bought with a great price.' What we have to offer Him, in worship and in love and in fellowship, is of value to Him, and He responds in bountiful measure.

Freedom to be ourselves

One night, after I had been speaking on this subject, one of the leaders in a particular church said to me, 'Tom, for the first time in years I now feel I can take a deep breath and just be myself.' You see, he had been trying, as so many of us do, to live up to other people's expectations of him. I knew what he had been going through. I, too, had once tried to project the correct image of a successful pastor of a flock. Terribly hard work, because it wasn't me, and doomed to failure because it wasn't true! Thankfully I have now discovered that I do not need to be anybody or anything but myself.

Denial of the self is not the submerging or denial of individuality: in actual fact, it is the restoration of the possibility of true individuality. We have already quoted Galatians 2:20. Let me paraphrase it for you to express what I believe was on the heart of the apostle: 'I, the self-centered one, have been crucified with Christ. Nevertheless I, the individual, lives; however, it is not the self-centered one, but in me, the individual, that Christ now lives.'

Let me show you something very beautiful in Colossians 3:4. The Concordant Literal translation reads as follows:

Whenever Christ, our Life, should be manifested, then you also shall be manifested together with him in glory.

In the context, the manifestation refers primarily to the Second Coming, but it also means something more immediate. It means that when Christ is manifested in our life, then we (that is the real person that we are), are manifested together with Him. He cannot, in fact, be manifested in us, unless we are willing to show our real selves. There is no way in which Christ can be seen in me, unless I am prepared to let my real self be seen also. If the real self is to be seen in this way, then there must be a continual reduction in those hidden areas that we shield from one another.

This does **not** mean that we are called upon to share all the details of our lives with everyone in our particular church or fellowship. It is heart attitude that is important, so we do not maintain or build protective barriers to shield off areas of weakness.

In any given situation, we must be guided by love and wisdom to know the extent to which we should share ourselves. In other words, we share with others at the level of openness **to which they can respond without feeling threatened.** Sharing at too deep a level with people who are not prepared for it can be a shattering – even destructive – experience for them.

But the simple honesty of being what we are is something else. The wonderful thing is that when we find the courage just to be ourselves, what is revealed is always much more beautiful than the image we were trying to project! More wonderful still, Christ always honors that self-revelation by revealing Himself together with us!

We find, also, a great deliverance from certain false attitudes that are commonplace among Christians. One is false humility – the inability to accept praise or commendation in a natural, gracious way. I have discovered a great liberation in the whole area of humility. Once I used to try hard to be humble, till I found myself getting quite proud about my humility. (It is a very humbling thing to discover that you are proud about being humble!) Thankfully, I have given all that away.

I have discovered that God is far more concerned than I am about the danger of pride. What is more, He can detect its appearance far sooner than I can, and when I need it He can prick my balloon and cut me down to size with devastating effectiveness. Because He really is the Good Shepherd, I can trust Him in this and similar areas of my life.

When we are free to be ourselves we become authentic, and because we are authentic we become credible, that is, believable. Never be afraid of showing your weaknesses as well as your strengths, your failures as well as your successes. A woman said something to me years ago that has been formative in my ministry. She said, 'You have helped us so much because we can identify with your weaknesses.' People do not identify with our strengths. They may admire our victories, but they cannot identify with them. Our failures they can identify with; and if out of those failures we have learned things in God, we have living truth to give them.

Freedom to love ourselves

When we are free to be ourselves, we are also free to love ourselves again – this time not as an end but as a means. Moreover, this is not just a rueful acceptance of the way we are, because we have no option but to put up with ourselves! It is genuine, positive regard for what we are, individuals whom God has made in His image and likeness.

We have already referred to the way in which the self as a goal-directed mechanism creates the self-image that dominates most of our attitude towards life. Many Christians are still inhibited by a very negative self-image. They feel unwanted, unworthy and unlovable. Faith becomes a difficult thing: God appears distant and stern and there is little real experience of the abundant, joyous life that Jesus said He came to bring.

Such people are really as self-centered as any others. They are locked in on themselves and on the inadequacies they see or imagine in themselves. But when the work of the cross and the power of the Holy Spirit sets them free from self-centeredness, they are free to discover the truth about themselves, and to find out what they are really like.

Remember the story of Jacob in the book of Genesis, realizing that in the Bible a name always means an identity. 'Jacob' means 'supplanter'; from his earliest years little Jacob grew up hearing his name and from it learning a self-image. We find that he lived out this self-image very consistently. He supplanted Esau out of his birthright, then he supplanted him out of his blessing, and then he went to Laban and supplanted Laban out of the best of his flocks. But finally Jacob came to the brook Jabbok, in desperation, because his self-image had led him to the brink of destruction. The great struggle, the wrestling with God, was over that very issue.

> *'What is your name* [self-image]*?'*
> *'Jacob* [Supplanter].*'*
> *'Your name* [self-image] *will no longer be Jacob*
>   [Supplanter], *but Israel* [Prince with God].*'*
>   (Genesis 32:27–28)

But before that happened, God had to touch Jacob's thigh and cripple the source of his prideful self-sufficiency.

▶ **It is only when self is deposed that with it can go the whole false self-image that has restricted and limited our growth. Only then are we free to receive from the Lord the understanding of our real identity.**

> *'...I will also give him a white stone with a new name written on it, known only to him who receives it.'*
>   (Revelation 2:17b)

The new name is a new identity; it is our true self-image. It is known only to each one of us individually, and to the Lord who reveals it. In the ground plan of every personality, the

Creator has formed a unique individuality. There are within us gifts and abilities and capabilities that in many cases are only potential, because they have never been realized. Now the Holy Spirit is able to breathe on these potentials, to give us faith to believe in them and by faith to bring them from the merely potential to the actual. This is why there is so often such a great flowering of creative activity in lives that have been filled with the Holy Spirit.

When we are in harmony with ourselves, when we are at ease with ourselves, when we love ourselves the way we are intended to, then we are at ease and in harmony with others, and able to offer them a relationship of life and love.

Freedom to be fulfilled

God the Father has placed in every person a drive to be fulfilled, for his or her full potential to be actualized. His purpose for all His children is that '... *speaking the truth in love, we will in all things grow up into him who is the Head, that is, Christ'* (Ephesians 4:15).

All that has gone before is prerequisite to fulfillment. It has been very truly said that 'the un-given self is the unfulfilled self.' Set free from self-centered living, we are free to give ourselves, to live openly towards others and towards life, to live with the walls down, and to reach out in faith and hope, offering others the gift of life that is in Christ.

This giving is often non-verbal. It is not necessary that there always be words, for if our hearts are open to people, and the protective walls between us are down, we offer them life.

> *'Whoever believes in me, as the Scripture has said, streams of living water will flow from within him.' By this he meant the Spirit, whom those who believed in him were later to receive...* (John 7:38–39)

I remember at a charismatic prayer meeting, talking to a Roman Catholic woman who had once worked with my wife. After moving to another town, she had come to know the Lord and to receive the baptism in the Holy Spirit. She said,

'There was always something about your wife that fascinated me. I wanted what she had, but I didn't know what it was. But now I know.' My wife says that as far as she can remember she never had a conversation with that woman about the Lord. But, you see, the river had been flowing. Once people feel its touch, I am convinced they receive an impression they never ever forget.

Of course, to live like that implies a real and certain vulnerability. People will not always receive and respond to what we offer them of ourselves, even when we offer them Christ and life, because there is death in the world. *'The wages of sin,'* Paul tells us, *'is death.'* This death is **now**, not just later on in eternity. So when life is offered, many times death will rise up and try to destroy it and us. At those times there will be hurt.

I was speaking about this once at a retreat for university students. A young woman came to me afterwards and said, 'What you say is impossible. You can't live like that towards everybody. You'd get hurt too much.' It's true, you **will** get hurt. Oh yes, that is unavoidable. The wonderful thing, however, is that you will never be destroyed. Do you know why? Because the life within you is **resurrection life**. It is the life of Christ that has already been through death, and come out in victory.

> *'For we know that since Christ was raised from the dead, he cannot die again; death no longer has mastery over him.'*
> (Romans 6:9)

Because of resurrection life within us, we can go on giving ourselves openly and 'recklessly', offering humanity life, because it has at last become flesh in us. In the process we grow up to maturity, fulfilling in the present time and on into eternity all that God has made us to be.

How the self comes into its own

It is now that the self really comes into its own. Remember how we described it – a goal-directed mechanism. Fixed on an object or a goal, it works to produce that in us. God's purpose for us is to conform us to the image of His Son. How does it actually happen?

The self does it. That source of so many of our problems – because it has been misplaced and loaded with a task for which it is totally unfitted – now works for us. Fixed on Christ, it will work day and night, consciously and unconsciously, by any and every means, to reproduce in us the likeness of Jesus. Isn't that fantastic! God not only chose the goal for our lives, He not only created the drive within us for fulfillment, He created the ego with the capability of bringing His purpose about. Our only requirement is that we keep it directed towards Jesus.

> *And we, who with unveiled faces all reflect the Lord's glory, are being transformed into his likeness with ever-increasing glory, which comes from the Lord, who is the Spirit.*
> (2 Corinthians 3:18)

That is how it works. Keep the self focused on fear, doubt, sin and failure, and it will reproduce them in us. It cannot do anything else. Keep it fixed on Jesus, and it will produce His likeness in us. It cannot do otherwise.

> *... Let us throw off everything that hinders and the sin that so easily entangles, and let us run with perseverance the race marked out for us. Let us fix our eyes on Jesus, the author and perfecter of our faith ...* (Hebrews 12:1–2)

The self, a poor master, turns out to be an efficient, untiring, effective servant, once it has been set free to assume its proper role.

It turns out that we achieve Christ-likeness not by striving or self-conscious modeling on His life. We become like Him just by being absorbed in Him. As we concentrate the core of our life on Jesus, as we contemplate His actions and meditate on His words, we – without being aware of it – are being changed into what we are focused upon.

Increasingly we will find what when we do things God's way, everything goes for us. The whole of life backs us up. We step into the flow of the universe, and the life of the Kingdom. In the long run we cannot but succeed. Do it our own way, let self get back again into the driving seat, and everything is against us. But the best, the freest, the most fulfilling way – because it accords with our true redeemed nature – is to go with God. We were made to fit His way of doing things. We were made in His image and in His likeness. The spiritual becomes increasingly natural – and the natural increasingly spiritual.

PART V

Chapter 18

Living Out of the Spirit

One of the most important principles for success in the Christian life is set out in the fifth chapter of the apostle Paul's epistle to the Galatians.

> *So, I say, live by the Spirit, and you will not gratify the desires of the sinful nature. For the sinful nature desires what is contrary to the Spirit, and the Spirit what is contrary to the sinful nature. They are in conflict with each other, so that you do not do what you want. But if you are led by the Spirit, you are not under law.* (Galatians 5:16–18)

> *Since we live by the Spirit, let us keep in step with the Spirit.* (Galatians 5:25)

Too often we overlook the order in which God puts things. Yet His order is always important. For example, in the above passage, the positive injunction (the thing we are to do) is to walk by the Spirit. If we walk by the Spirit, the outcome or natural result is that we will not carry out the desires of the flesh.

Usually we turn it round the other way. We make strenuous efforts not to carry out the desires of the flesh, hoping that, if we succeed, we will then be able to walk in the Spirit. Satan encourages this approach. He delights in getting us tied up in a long, bitter war of attrition against the flesh, secure in the knowledge that we will ultimately end up defeated and discouraged.

Why do we persist in trying it this way? One reason is that most of us have only vague ideas of what it means to live in the Spirit – and no idea of how to go about it! Nor are preachers often very much help. They make it sound very desirable and spiritual, but how to actually do it is seldom spelled out. On the other hand, we know only too well what it means to carry out the desires of the flesh. This enemy has familiar features. Usually, therefore, we stick with the battle we know and end up again and again with the familiar taste of defeat in our mouths.

But need it always end like this? If it is true that victory is to be found not by battling with the flesh but by walking by the Spirit, surely it is worth any effort to find the way into such a walk. That is the purpose of this study: not so much to explore the beauty and power of the Spirit-filled life as to clarify the basic 'how to do it' principles. We shall also find exciting discoveries, because they open a window both into the eternal purposes of the heart of God and also into the mysteries of our own created being.

The making of humanity

As we have pointed out several times already, the Bible reveals that all people, created in the image of God, are a tri-unity: spirit, soul and body.

> *May God himself, the God of peace, sanctify you through and through. May your whole spirit, soul and body be kept blameless at the coming of our Lord Jesus Christ.*
>
> (1 Thessalonians 5:23)

Now, however, we need to explore much more fully the significance of this basic insight into the nature of humanity.

In the first chapters of Genesis we find what are usually considered to be two separate accounts of the creation of humanity. We are going to see, however, that these are not two different accounts at all but one unified statement as to our origin and our essential nature. Turn first to Genesis 1:27:

> *So God created man in his own image, in the image of God he created him; male and female he created them. God blessed them...*

The Hebrew word here translated 'created' is *bara*. It has been said that *bara* expresses better than any other verb the idea of an absolute creation, or creation *ex nihilo* (that is, out of nothing). It is used exclusively in the Old Testament for God's activity. It is never used to refer to the activity of human beings.

We know for example that God created Adam out of nothing. Furthermore He created us in His own image and after His own likeness. What is God like? Jesus tells us in John 4:24 that *'God is Spirit.'* The question then is this, 'When God created man and woman, what did He make out of nothing that was in the image and likeness of His own Spirit-Being?' The answer is that **Genesis 1 records the creation by God of the human spirit**.

When we turn to Genesis 2:7, we read something quite different:

> *... the Lord God formed the man from the dust of the ground and breathed into his nostrils the breath of life, and the man became a living being.*

The Hebrew word for 'formed' is not *bara* but *yatsar*, which means 'created out of already existing substance'. So, God formed Adam's body out of dust.

Then we must ask, 'What was it that God breathed into the body He had formed?' In Hebrew the same word means both 'breath' and 'spirit'. So Genesis 2:7 tells us that God formed that first human body out of an existing substance, and into it He breathed mankind's spirit that He had created out of nothing.

Finally, we learn from this passage that when this spirit entered Adam's body, his soul-life came into being. He became, as Ferrar Fenton translates Genesis 2:19, *'the man with the living soul.'* Not only does the spirit give life to the body – *'for the body without the spirit is dead'* (James 2:26) – but the relationship between the spirit and the body creates the soul, that is our rational, emotional and volitional faculties: our mind, emotion and will. The human spirit and soul are thus from the beginning essentially different both in nature and in function. The difference is of such fundamental importance that we must examine it in a little more detail.

The role of the human spirit

In all people, the human spirit, made in the image and likeness of God, was intended to fulfill a two-fold function.

▶   **1. The role of the human spirit was to relate us to God and so enable us to receive from God both life and wisdom.**

The relationship with God is what the Bible calls *'life'*. When the Bible speaks of life and death it always speaks of relationship, not existence. To be rightly related to the living God is life, to be cut off from him is death. We may in this death state still exist, still walk around, laugh, fight, cry and work; but we are dead because we no longer have any correspondence with God the source of life.

A person's spirit was also intended to give him access to divine wisdom, to order and direct his life.

> **It is essential to grasp that no person was ever meant to have within himself – independently of God – the resources of wisdom to enable him or her to make a success of life.**

Lack of wisdom is humanity's great problem today. We are brilliantly clever; but without wisdom this very cleverness becomes destructive. Thus a secular writer recently characterized the human race rather sadly in these terms: 'Mankind is, after all, nothing more than a particularly clever, particularly mischievous species of monkey.'

What is wisdom?

Wisdom is the ability to choose the right goals and to achieve those goals by the best means.

The Bible tells us two things about it. Firstly, the source of wisdom is in God alone.

> ...*Praise be to the name of God for ever and ever; wisdom and power are his.* (Daniel 2:20)

> *The LORD gave Solomon wisdom, just as he had promised him.* (1 Kings 5:12)

Secondly, because it comes from God and therefore must be received from Him, wisdom in a person is always located in the heart, not the head; in the spirit, not the mind. Therefore it has no necessary dependence on either intelligence or education.

> *Now Joshua son of Nun was filled with the spirit of wisdom...* (Deuteronomy 34:9)

> ...*that the God of our Lord Jesus Christ, the glorious Father, may give you the Spirit of wisdom and revelation, so that you may know him better.* (Ephesians 1:17)

▶ **2. Because of its access to divine wisdom, the human spirit was that part of a person's being which exercised rule and direction over his or her life.**

In unfallen Adam, his mind ruled his body, his spirit ruled his mind, and the Holy Spirit ruled his spirit. In that divine order he was a perfectly whole being with no breach in his nature through which sickness or sin could enter. Not only was Adam a whole being, he was also God-centered and therefore perfectly balanced. With his spirit in control, relating him to the living center of the universe, all his faculties and drives were held in perfect harmony and beautiful balance.

One of the perennial problems in the Church has always been the problem of balance. It is still the case, even where the Holy Spirit has been touching the church. This is because in so many Christians the recognition of the spirit as the governing center of the individual life has been lost – and with it the realization of the presence of the Holy Spirit as the creative center and the balance of the corporate life of the Body.

The role of the human soul

There is sometimes a tendency among proponents of 'deeper life' teaching to denigrate the human soul. Something is described as 'soulish', as though soulish is necessarily evil. It suggests that the soul creates so many problems for the spiritual life that we would be far better off without it altogether. What in fact is often suggested is that it is possible to get out of the soulish realm altogether and live entirely in the spirit. This is not only impossible, it is a grave misunderstanding of what the Bible really teaches. True, the soul has and creates problems, because it has been damaged by sin. But God made it and, indeed, it seems part of the makeup of a person that is particularly dear to the heart of God.

The function of the soul in a person, as we have seen from Genesis 2:7, is to relate his or her inner spiritual being to the outer flesh-and-blood being. In other words, the soul incarnates an individual's spiritual life in bodily form and expression. This principle of incarnation is distinctive to the human race and to it alone. There are created beings that inhabit the spiritual realm: the angels, evil spirits and so on. There are also created beings that inhabit the material realm: that is, the orders of the animal kingdom.

Humanity is unique in that we inhabit both the material and spiritual realms. And it is our soul faculties, because they link spirit and body, which were to be the means for us to introduce the values and realities of the spiritual realm into the realm of nature. Through humanity, God purposed to share His own love-nature with creation, and it was for this purpose that human beings were given dominion.

> *It is not to angels that he has subjected the world to come, about which we are speaking. But there is a place where someone has testified: 'What is man that you are mindful of him, the son of man that you care for him? You made him a little lower than the angels; you crowned him with glory and honor . . . '* (Hebrews 2:5–7)

When the angels fell, God, as far as our revelation goes, made no provision for their redemption. But when humanity sinned, so greatly was God committed to those who were made in His image, that He went to the amazing length of joining with fallible creatures and dying at their hands to redeem them.

> *Since the children have flesh and blood, he too shared in their humanity so that by his death he might destroy him who holds the power of death – that is, the devil – and free those who all their lives were held in slavery by their fear of death.* (Hebrews 2:14–15)

Human beings pride themselves upon the faculties of their soul-life; and that, as we shall see, is often its greatest problem. But these same faculties are also our glory, which is why the Son of God died to redeem us. They have been perfectly displayed just once as a prototype of what they were always meant to be. In the last Adam the eternal Son Himself entered a human body and a human nature.

> *Therefore, when Christ came into the world, he said:*
> *'Sacrifice and offering you did not desire,*
> *but a body you prepared for me . . . '* (Hebrews 10:5)

The soul-life that was displayed in the body caused John to write,

The Word became flesh and made his dwelling among us. We have seen his glory, the glory of the One and Only, who came from the Father, full of grace and truth.

(John 1:14)

Chapter 19

Subverted Man

As we have seen, we were never intended to have the resource of wisdom within ourselves; instead we were to have access through our spirit to God's wisdom. The temptation in the Garden of Eden centered on this very issue. Satan's advice to Eve was to reach across the boundary set by God and seize the resources of wisdom for herself. That way there would be no more need for dependence on God.

Eve was deceived – and the whole human race after her. Wisdom was **not** in the tree of the knowledge of good and evil after all. Satan lied. All time wisdom was where it had always been, in the tree of life, that is Christ: *'in whom are hidden all the treasures of wisdom and knowledge'* (Colossians 2:3).

The tree of the knowledge of good and evil brought not wisdom but death. Humanity was driven out of the Garden, henceforth denied access to the tree of life – and its wisdom – until the Redeemer comes, and through another tree on Calvary, opens a door for us to return. But in the meantime, fallen humanity strives to live by its own wisdom. It chooses goals but they are motivated by selfish ambition and sordid jealousy. It devises means to attain its goals but falls prey to a 'wisdom' that is earthly, unspiritual and demonic (James 3:15). This so-called wisdom not only fails to bring knowledge of God, but leads to extremes of folly – ultimately, to actually crucifying the Lord of glory.

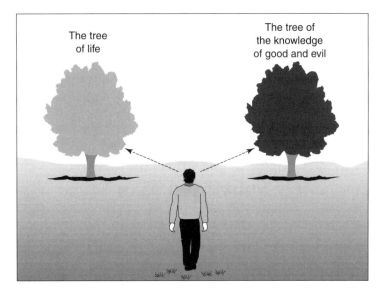

Figure 18: Where is wisdom to be found?

The spirit dethroned

When Adam and Eve sinned, not only did they lose access to divine wisdom, but the divine order in their natures fell into ruin. Their spirit, cut off from God, lost its power and authority. At the same time the tree of the knowledge of good and evil inflated their soul powers and physical appetites. The progressive outworking of this act of sin has been to shift the dominant place in human nature. This place of dominance is now assumed by either soulish or physical faculties.

Some people are ruled by a powerful intellect, others are at the mercy of a strong emotional nature, or a masterful will, and others still are dominated by bodily appetites or physical drives. The result is always ruinous, because neither soul nor body was ever meant to rule, nor is either capable of doing so. What eventually results is a continual power struggle between competing desires, all clamoring for satisfaction and all claiming to be paramount. The individual ends up hopelessly at war with his or herself, divided and unbalanced, a slave of the sin that is within.

Remember that the human spirit still exists, and still functions. Death means that the spirit has lost its link with God, the source of life, but it is still there – although in no better shape than the rest of the person's nature. Created to relate to an external source of power and authority, the individual's spirit has fallen under the domination of Satan.

As for you, you were dead in your transgressions and sins, in which you used to live when you followed the ways of this world and of the ruler of the kingdom of the air, the spirit who is now at work in those who are disobedient.

(Ephesians 2:1–2)

The unregenerate person still has a functioning human spirit, and with it can have genuine spiritual experiences. Such a person can with their spirit contact the spiritual realm; but because they are cut off from God by sin, the only spirit realm they can reach is the realm that is also in the state of death. You must realize this, because there are many spiritual experiences available today that come from the realm of death and have nothing to do with God. Not only do they include spiritism, the occult and pagan religions, but also idolatry in all of its ancient and modern forms. Behind all of them there is demonic activity seeking after a person's spirit, not to give life, but to suck it dry.

Add that person's disease-ridden body to the picture, and you cannot but cry with Isaiah:

...Your whole head is injured, your whole heart afflicted. From the sole of your foot to the top of your head there is no soundness – only wounds and bruises and open sores...

(Isaiah 1:5–6)

Chapter 20

Converted Man

All people need to be converted because, in a real sense, they have become subverted. They each need conversion to turn them right side up again. The good news of the gospel is that, in the fullness of time, Christ came: the last Adam, a life-giving Spirit, to regenerate our spirit-being. In the experience of the new birth, each human spirit is re-created and restored to a life-relationship with God. When we are born again, what part of us is affected? Not our body, nor our soul, but our spirit:

> *Flesh gives birth to flesh, but the Spirit gives birth to spirit.*
> (John 3:6)

God the Father is the Father of the spirit of each one of us (Hebrews 12:9) and it is this spirit that is '... *created to be like God in true righteousness and holiness'* (Ephesians 4:24).

But redemption does not stop with the spirit. Christ died to redeem the whole person, but He does it in accordance with the economy of the person's original creation. That original creation was not a mistake: it was a perfect design. And redemption does not do violence to that design. Two stages are therefore necessarily involved in salvation, as far as human nature is concerned.

1. Not only is the human spirit restored to a life-relationship with God; it is to be restored to its place of primacy over soul and body.

2. The soul, to be saved, must come to the cross – not to be destroyed but to yield up its claim to rule. Only thus can it be liberated.

> *For whoever wants to save his* [soul-]*life will lose it, but whoever loses his* [soul-] *life for me will find it. What good will it be for a man if he gains the whole world, yet forfeits his* soul[-life]? *Or what can a man give in exchange for his* soul[-life]?   (Matthew 16:25–26)

When the soul-life loses itself (that is, lays down its right to rule), and the human spirit is filled with the Holy Spirit, the power of the Spirit is released from within the human spirit to sanctify and harmonize the faculties of the soul and to heal the body. Members of the Catholic charismatic movement use a term they themselves have coined for the baptism in the Holy Spirit. They call it 'the release of the Spirit.' They have touched with true spiritual instinct on one of the most vital aspects of the baptism in the Spirit – the all-pervasive nature of the experience. The power of the Holy Spirit, and the authority of the Holy Spirit, were always intended by God to be mediated through all of a person's life, but in this order:

1. the spirit
2. the soul
3. the body.

> *...And if anyone does not have the Spirit of Christ, he does not belong to Christ. But if Christ is in you, your spirit is alive because of righteousness.*   (Romans 8:9–10)

> *The mind of sinful man is death, but the mind controlled by the Spirit is life and peace.*   (Romans 8:6)

> *And if the Spirit of him who raised Jesus from the dead is living in you, he who raised Christ from the dead will also give life to your mortal bodies through his Spirit, who lives in you.*   (Romans 8:11)

Do you see the divine order?

1. The **spirit** is **alive**.
2. The **mind** is **life** and peace
3. **Life** is given to the mortal **body**.

The aim in the rest of this study is to show how this truth can be translated into actual experience.

Chapter 21

The Functions
of the Human Spirit

We have discovered that the God-intended role for the human spirit, restored by the new birth and empowered by the Holy Spirit, is to exercise rule and direction over the soul and, through the soul, over the body. But for this to have practical significance and meaning for us we need first to meet and recognize our own human spirit. I say this advisedly, because until I was baptized in the Holy Spirit I was not even aware, as a matter of experience, that I had a human spirit that was different from my mind.

The spirit and soul are immaterial aspects of a person: that is, we do not see either of them. We know them only as we experience their functioning. I know my soul, not because I am aware of its functioning as mind, emotion and will: I think, I feel and I decide. When I am doing any of these things I am living out of my soul.

The spirit, like the soul, has three functions, and as we shall see later in Figure 19 (p. 187) they relate in a direct, but not exclusive, way to the three functions of the soul. When we are aware of these functions or when we are doing these things, we are living out of our spirit.

Knowledge

The first function of the human spirit is knowledge, but it is knowledge of a particular kind. It is direct knowledge that comes intuitively – not as the result of rational, deductive mental processes. It is important to grasp that in this sense we do not know with our mind. We understand with our mind but we **know** with our spirit.

> *For who among men knows the thoughts of a man except the man's spirit within him? In the same way no one knows the thoughts of God except the Spirit of God. We have not received the spirit of the world but the Spirit who is from God, that we may understand what God has freely given us.*
> (1 Corinthians 2:11–12)

The interesting thing is that few great discoveries of science have ever been made by the deductive method, that is the gathering of data, the ordering of data into classifications, and the deduction of laws from data. All of the greatest of human discoveries have been made by intuitive insights. In their spirit people have 'seen' truth; then they have set up experiments to prove or disprove what they have intuitively known.

Women are generally much more familiar with this kind of knowledge than are men, although there are also many intuitive men. The only problem is when people think their intuition is infallible! Human intuition is not infallible – but it is spiritual; it is the human spirit receiving knowledge. Because we are finite and damaged by sin, we perceive knowledge imperfectly and often misinterpret what we perceive.

Knowledge of God

One of the most life-changing things in my own experience has been to discover that we relate to God with the same faculties we use in relating to other people. This is often not understood and therefore needs emphasizing. God is a person, and our relationship with Him is a personal one, therefore we use the same faculties in knowing God and relating to Him as we use in knowing and relating to any other person.

You cannot know a person fully through your senses and your mind. A person is known directly and intuitively with the spirit. Some people you can reach and know in this way in a matter of minutes. Other people you somehow can't reach at all. I have heard wives say, 'I've been married twenty years, but I don't know my husband.' Or parents say, 'I can't seem to be able to reach my children. I feel I don't know them at all.' It is the spirit that is frustrated, because it can't get the knowledge it wants.

It is vital to understand that knowledge of God comes in this direct, intuitive way. We may not be able to explain or describe how we know but we can 'just know' in a certain and unshakable way that God has spoken to us, that God has heard our prayer, or that we are in the presence of God. Many times, because we do not understand this, we are not aware that it is God who has been speaking to us.

Over the years I have asked many people, hundreds of them by now, and I have never found one who, on reflection, could not remember some direct, intuitive experience that they now realize was actually an approach from God. The tragedy is that we have made the Christian faith so much a matter of head knowledge that these experiences of the human spirit have been almost totally neglected.

We must also realize that knowledge of God coming to the human spirit (and not to the mind) is not God choosing to do it in the most difficult way possible for us. It is God doing it in the only way possible. God wants to communicate to us not mere information, but knowledge that is life.

> *Now this is eternal life: that they may know you, the only true God, and Jesus Christ, whom you have sent.*
> (John 17:3)

The mind cannot receive life: it can only handle information or data. Only a person's spirit is able to receive life. Therefore only the spirit is able to receive knowledge of God that is also the communication of life. In some measure it is true – even on a mere human level – that to know a person is to experience life. When someone has really shared his or her self with you, however brief the encounter, you feel more alive, more alert, more full. There has been an impartation of life from the other person's spirit. When that impartation is from the living God who shares himself with us, there is an experience of eternal life.

Conscience

The second function of the human spirit that we have to consider is conscience. We are all familiar with its operation, although we may not have recognized that it is not to be equated with the mind.

> ...*to those who are corrupted and do not believe, nothing is pure. In fact, both their minds and consciences are corrupted.*
> (Titus 1:15)

Conscience is not the voice of God, although the voice of God speaks to our conscience. Conscience is a function of the human spirit. It has been created with the ability to 'see' general moral truths (such as honesty and faithfulness) and the ability to apply them to particular cases so that we tell the truth – even at some cost – and keep our promises – even when it is inconvenient to do so.

To understand how conscience functions, we must distinguish its form and its content.

- **Form** is the way that conscience works. This is the same for everybody, regardless of race, sex, age, background or culture. It tells us **when** we are doing right and **when** we are doing wrong.

  > ...*they show that the requirements of the law are written on their hearts, their consciences also bearing witness, and their thoughts now accusing, now even defending them.*
  > (Romans 2:15)

- **Content** is the basis on which conscience makes its judgments. It tells us **what** is right and **what** is wrong. The content of conscience varies with culture, age, background and learning, so that one person's conscience may condemn him or her for something that another's conscience is neutral about, or even approves.

On the other hand, when the Holy Spirit awakens the human spirit and displays to the conscience the value-standards of God's holiness and love, conviction of sin – that can lead to repentance – takes place. When there is genuine repentance, the work of the Holy Spirit is to point to the efficacy of the blood of Calvary to deal with the guilt of sin and to speak peace to the troubled conscience.

> *Therefore, brothers, since we have confidence to enter the Most Holy Place by the blood of Jesus ... let us draw near to God with a sincere heart in full assurance of faith, having our hearts sprinkled to cleanse us from a guilty conscience...*
> (Hebrews 10:19–22)

Obedience to conscience is fundamental to moral behavior. In sanctification the continuing work of the Holy Spirit is to write the law of God upon the heart, so that the spirit, looking into that gracious law of liberty, becomes increasingly sensitive, leading to authentic purity of behavior and motivation.

There is another extremely important function of conscience that is seldom appreciated but needs to be understood today as never before: **it bears witness to truth.** Grasp hold of this: essentially, truth or falsehood registers on conscience, not on the mind. You can hear a story that is so plausible that you are unable to fault it, but somehow you just 'know' that it is suspect. Another person tells a completely unsupported tale with quite improbable features but you 'know' he is telling the truth. What knows truth and error? The conscience. You find an example in Romans 9:1 where Paul says, *'I speak the truth in Christ – I am not lying, my conscience confirms it in the Holy Spirit.'* Therefore apostolic preaching was not directed at the minds of the hearers, but at their conscience. The apostles knew that you do not need to prove truth, you only have to declare it, because it carries its own in-built validation – to the conscience.

> *... we have renounced secret and shameful ways; we do not use deception, nor do we distort the word of God. On the contrary, by setting forth the truth plainly we commend ourselves to every man's conscience in the sight of God.*
>
> (2 Corinthians 4:2)

I remember one time speaking at a Christian businessmen's meeting to which a large number of unbelievers had been invited. At the beginning I said to them, 'I am going to show you an infallible way to find out whether what I am saying tonight is true or not.' That caught their attention all right! Then I said, 'Just notice how it registers on your conscience.' You could feel them buckle at the middle. The objections and intellectual difficulties people throw up against the gospel are, most of the time, to protect the conscience from the assault of truth.

In fact, it is impossible to over-stress the importance of maintaining a clean conscience. Paul said he strove *'to keep my conscience clear before God and man'* (Acts 24:16). Only a conscience that is kept clean by the blood of Jesus is able accurately to bear witness to truth. I suspect that if you traced back every heresy that has ever plagued the church of God, you would find somewhere in the beginning a defiled conscience that was unable to discern truth from error. In the deceptions of the last days – which the Bible warns us about – a clear conscience is likely to be our best safeguard.

> *The Spirit clearly says that in later times some will abandon the faith and follow deceiving spirits and things taught by demons. Such teachings come through hypocritical liars, whose consciences have been seared as with a hot iron.*
>
> (1 Timothy 4:1–2)

Communication

The third function of the human spirit is worship or communion. We could put this more simply by calling it communication. Jesus said to the woman of Samaria, *'God is spirit, and his worshippers must worship in spirit and truth'* (John 4:24).

Not only do we **communicate** with God **only with our spirit**, but we communicate with one another in the same way. If I do not reach out in my spirit and somehow touch the other person's spirit, there is no real communication. I may transmit data or information that may be understood, but there is no communication between us as persons.

I first discovered this when I used to help run a Teen Challenge youth club in Wellington. There was a boy, who came in quite regularly, called 'Grubby' – a name that fitted him quite well. His regular routine when bored – which was often – was to annoy and irritate everybody in sight, including me. His inventiveness was virtually inexhaustible, and his success rate was impressive. One particular Friday night Grubby had tried my patience almost beyond endurance. I was sitting down by myself with a cup of coffee, struggling to retain my spirituality, when he sauntered over and, with an air of triumphant insolence on his face, positioned himself right opposite me.

Suddenly the Holy Spirit within me reached out to the boy. I know it was the Holy Spirit because in myself all I was feeling was annoyance and sulky hurt. Besides, in those days, I didn't even know how to reach out to people. I found myself saying, 'Graham, tell me why you behave like that. I don't think you're really like that at all.' Suddenly I found I had touched his spirit. For the next hour he sat there and poured out all his frustrations, his terrible home life, his loneliness and his failures. And never ever after that did he cause me a moment's trouble. Right there I learned that only when we reach out in our spirit and touch the other person's spirit can we really help them.

Many, many people do not know how to communicate. Husband and wives have been married for years – but don't know how to communicate. It's not that they don't speak to one another. They may have said millions of words – many perhaps better unsaid – but there has been no communication. I remember one woman, married 23 years, whose husband came home from work one night and said, 'It's all over – if there ever was anything. I'm leaving.' She said to me, 'We never fell out, or got mad at each other. We just lived within ourselves, and in the end there was just nothing there.' Children say, 'I can't communicate with my parents.' What do they mean? Not that they talk a different language, but that they find no spirit reaching out in love to them; or when they reach out to their parents there is nothing that responds.

The wonderful thing about God is that when we reach out in our spirit to Him we always communicate, because He is always reaching out in His Spirit to us. The Holy Spirit *'goes out from the Father'* (John 15:26). If in our prayer we do not reach out in our spirit, there is no communication: we are just 'saying our prayers.' On the other hand, if we reach out in our spirit there can be genuine communication without words at all.

> *In the same way, the Spirit helps us in our weakness. We do not know what we ought to pray for, but the Spirit himself intercedes for us with groans that words cannot express.*
> (Romans 8:26)

We cannot share the life of Christ or our knowledge of Him apart from sharing our own spirit also. Most of our failures in personal evangelism or Christian counseling are due to this. To be a channel for the Holy Spirit means that my human spirit has to become the 'carrier wave' on which the power and grace of the Holy Spirit can travel. If I am not willing to give myself to the other person, I cannot give him Christ.

Chapter 22

Relating Spirit and Soul

We are now beginning to recognize the difference between the nature and functioning of soul and spirit, not only theologically but also as experience. A key verse in Hebrews will help us.

> *For the word of God is living and active. Sharper than any double-edged sword, it penetrates even to dividing soul and spirit...* (Hebrews 4:12)

In other words, our spirit is the part of us to which the living word of God speaks, either giving direct intuitive knowledge, or witnessing to our conscience, or drawing out responsive worship.

We come now to a very vital but almost totally unexplored area: **the relationship between a person's spirit and soul.**

Clearly, if the human spirit is to be the center of rule and direction in the personality, it must relate in a particular way to the soul and the body. Furthermore, if our spirit is the dwelling place of the Holy Spirit, it is important to know how to open channels for the grace and power of the Spirit to flow out from our spirit to areas of need within soul and body.

Figure 19 shows two essential characteristics of our life in the Spirit.

Firstly, each function of the spirit of an individual is intended to relate in a particular way to one of the functions of the soul. Thus:

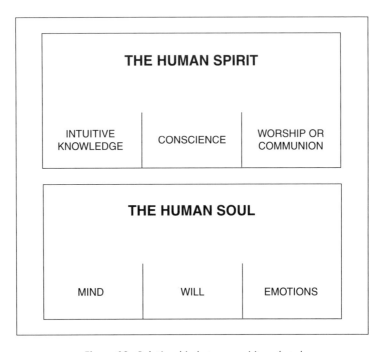

Figure 19: *Relationship between spirit and soul*

- Knowledge received in the spirit is meant to rule over the reasoning of the mind;
- The conscience is intended to direct and control the decisions of the will; and,
- The function of communion is to rule over the emotions.

Secondly, although the Holy Spirit resides in the human spirit, He will go no further without the desire and consent of the human will. That is why it is possible for us to quench the Spirit. We can say 'No!' to the Spirit of God and, omnipotent though He is, He will not force His way into the closed areas of our life anymore than He will force His way into the heart of an unbeliever. Dwelling within our spirit, the Spirit lives by His own law of vulnerable love. He can be provoked, grieved or made joyful; He can be inhibited or given freedom to act by our behavior and our response towards Him.

Now let us examine the principles by which spirit and soul relate to one another, so that we can begin to understand what it means to live out of our spirit – and thereby live by the power of the Holy Spirit.

Spirit, mind and faith

We have already seen that when God speaks to us, either directly or through His word, knowledge reaches our spirit. We call this knowledge **revelation**.

> 'No eye has seen,
>   no ear has heard,
>   no mind has conceived
>   what God has prepared for those who love him' –
> but God has revealed it to us by his Spirit.

(1 Corinthians 2:9–10)

▶ **When this knowledge is received intuitively in the spirit, then the possibility of faith arises.**

The link between mind and spirit is faith. This is shown in Figure 20. We must understand what faith is. Sometimes we have the idea, like Alice in Wonderland, that faith is 'believing three impossible things before breakfast.' Faith is not a leap in the dark, nor is it believing without evidence. Faith always produces results, because faith rests on knowledge.

Before I was a Christian I often used to think, 'If I only knew, then I would be able to believe.' After I became a Christian I thought, 'I was wrong. You believe first, then you know.' Now I realize I was actually right the first time: first you know and then you believe.

What we have to understand, however, is that the knowledge on which faith rests is a particular kind of knowledge. It is the direct, intuitive knowledge that comes from God to our spirit. Our rational mind has difficulty with that kind of knowledge.

> *The man without the Spirit does not accept the things that come from the Spirit of God, for they are foolishness to him,*

and he cannot understand them, because they are spiritually
discerned.   (1 Corinthians 2:14)

Therefore, when divine knowledge comes to our spirit, we
have to choose between trusting that knowledge – which is
the exercise of faith – or mistrusting – which is unbelief.

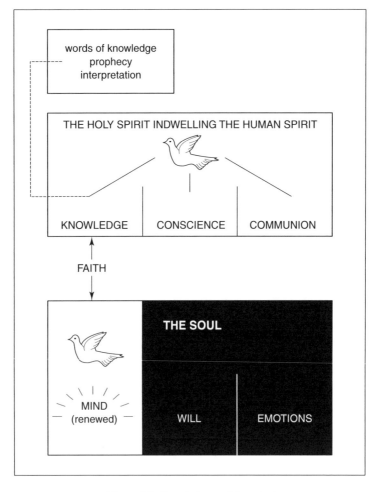

Figure 20: *Knowledge and the mind*

When we respond in faith, the power of the Holy Spirit is released from our spirit into our mind and beyond. In a sense, the amount of faith is not the essential element. It may be very small. After all, a fuse or switch is very small but the function it fulfills in completing the connection is very important. That is why Jesus says that if you have faith *'as small as a mustard seed'*, dramatic results can follow.

On the other hand, we can see the serious nature of unbelief. It is not just an amiable weakness that afflicts all Christians, it is the rejection of revelation knowledge, and an insuperable barrier to the flow of the Holy Spirit in our lives. The writer to the Hebrews draws attention to the generation of Israelites who had received the promise of entering into the land of Canaan yet died in the wilderness. He warns us that to receive a promise is not of itself enough.

> *For we also have had the gospel preached to us, just as they did; but the message they heard was of no value to them, because those who heard did not combine it faith.*
>
> (Hebrews 4:2)

If we reject the word of God through unbelief – truth though it is – it will never come to fruition in our lives.

Spiritual intuitions

There is a passage in Matthew chapter 18 where Jesus called a child to Him, stood him in the midst of those gathered there and said to His disciples,

> *'I tell you the truth, unless you change and become like little children, you will never enter the kingdom of heaven.'*
>
> (Matthew 18:3)

I was never very satisfied with the usual interpretations given to this passage – for example, that we are to become humble and trusting as little children. I know some children that are not a bit humble and who wouldn't trust you as far as they could see you on a dark night!

I do not think the real thrust of what Jesus meant was that at all. If you go into a home where there is a little toddler, he has you summed up in about fifteen seconds flat! He does it intuitively because he doesn't have much intellectual data about you – and anyway he probably wouldn't understand it! He makes up his mind about you solely on the basis of what his spirit tells him.

The interesting thing about a little child is that he goes one hundred per cent along with what his intuition tells him. If he decides he doesn't like you, you can't get near him. You may be wreathed in smiles and laden with goodies, but nothing will get him out from behind his mother's skirts or from under the kitchen table. On the other hand, if he decides he does like you, you can't get rid of him. He'll be all over you, sticky fingers and all; and if you won't let him put his half-eaten toffee in your mouth he'll poke it up your nose or in your left ear, so greatly does he want to share with you everything he has.

Do you understand what Jesus is saying?

▶   **Unless we are willing, like children, to trust the divine knowledge we receive in our spirit, we will never understand the ways of the kingdom of God.**

That is what walking in the Spirit means in the realm of the mind.

You are visiting someone with terminal cancer. You go to pray a comforting prayer and as you reach out to the Lord He unexpectedly says in your spirit, *'These signs shall follow them that believe: they shall lay hands on the sick and they shall recover. Do it.'* You know intuitively that it is a word from God for the sick person. But then your mind intervenes and says, 'You can't risk that! It's cancer. What happens if he doesn't get healed?' At that point faith or unbelief takes over. Either the mind ties you down to the physical data – a body dying of cancer – or faith reaches out to the new data from God that there is healing for the sick body. Faith disregards sense knowledge because it has access to higher knowledge: the knowledge of God's will and God's ability in this particular situation.

The importance of the mind

But the mind is not just a hindrance to the human spirit. It is very important in its own right. One of the greatest lacks in the church today is the absence of a Christian mind, the lack of an authentically Christian way of thinking about things. The function of the mind is to receive revelation knowledge from the spirit **in words**, or propositional statements, so that we can both appropriate what we have received and share it with others. In 1 Corinthians 2, Paul explains that revelation comes from the Spirit of God to the spirit of a person; but then he says:

> *This is what we speak, not in words taught us by human wisdom but in words taught by the Spirit, expressing spiritual truths in spiritual words.* (1 Corinthians 2:13)

There is a very important principle here. Revelation to an individual's spirit comes often as a flash of illumination. We 'see' something in God. But often what we 'see' in this way we find hard to explain even to ourselves. It can be virtually incommunicable.

Coming home from church one Sunday morning, my wife got into the car, very excited. She said, 'In the communion this morning I suddenly saw something wonderful about the name of Jesus.' I said, 'Marvelous! Tell us what it was.' She said, 'Oh, I couldn't put it in words, but it was wonderful!' Now, that was genuine revelation, but it had gone only halfway. Whenever inner illumination comes, we need to say, 'Lord, now I want to understand it in words, so I can obey it, and so I can pass it on to others.' Unless we do, the most wonderful experience of God can, as it were, run through our fingers and be lost.

Renewal of the mind

The mind also needs to be renewed to be able to properly judge and understand the intuitions of the spirit. Handling the intuitions of the spirit with an unrenewed mind can be disastrous. Nevertheless, every time we trust the word that comes to our spirit, faith releases the power of the Holy Spirit, from the spirit into the mind. When this becomes our habitual response the mind becomes *'controlled by the Spirit'* and this, Romans 8:6 tells us, is life and peace for the mind. We have dealt elsewhere at some length on the renewal of the mind, but here we can see how it actually takes place. The Holy Spirit, who knows the mind of God, comes alongside our mind to lift it into the ability to think God's thoughts after Him.

Concerning spiritual gifts

Next we have to see what light the last section throws on the operation of the spiritual gifts.

Firstly, it confirms the nature of these manifestations as *'spiritual gifts'* (1 Corinthians 12:1). A spiritual gift is a manifestation of the Holy Spirit to the human spirit, then from the human spirit to the mind.

Secondly, it illustrates the place of faith in the operation of spiritual gifts.

Word of knowledge

A **word of knowledge** is a word of divine knowledge that reveals, to the person to whom it is given, information about a situation or a person he does not know and could not naturally discover. Because it is revelation it comes directly and intuitively, and therefore faith is needed to step out on it. One of the first times I had a word of knowledge in a public meeting was at a gathering of Catholic and Anglican prayer groups. Just as I was about to give the altar call, the Lord showed me the details of the marriage of a person in that meeting. It was very serious, much more than just an ordinary marital problem.

I took a look at the size of the congregation and my mind told me, 'If you say that, you could end up with a hundred discontented wives at the front.' I was faithless. I listened to my mind and merely gave a general invitation for folk to come forward for prayer. The first woman up at the front told me the situation in her marriage. I already knew it. I was so rebuked because that dear woman was meant to know, while she was still in her seat, that the Lord knew the detail of her need and was able to meet it.

Prophecy and the interpretation of tongues

These spiritual gifts can also be understood from the model we have been discussing. Revelation, we have seen, is illumination from the Holy Spirit to the human spirit. A person receiving an utterance in tongues in a meeting is therefore expressing a revelation received in the spirit but not understood in the mind.

> *For if I pray in a tongue, my spirit prays, but my mind is unfruitful.*   (1 Corinthians 14:14)

So that those in a meeting receive understanding of what the Spirit is saying, the companion gift of interpretation has to come into operation. What is received in the spirit is then expressed in words.

In the gift of prophecy both stages take place within one person. The human spirit receives revelation, communicates it to the mind in words, and a word of prophecy is spoken. That is why Paul says,

> *He who prophesies is greater than one who speaks in tongues, unless he interprets, so that the church may be edified.*
> (1 Corinthians 14:5)

In both prophecy and the interpretation of tongues the element of faith is needed.

Usually only the beginning of the message, perhaps only one or two words, will be received by the mind. Only when the person steps out in faith on those few words will the flow from the spirit to the mind be released and the rest of the prophecy received. If you don't step out in faith and speak, the word is quenched and you may never be sure whether you really had a word from God at all. On the other hand, once the word of prophecy ceases in our spirit, we had better stop, too – even if it is in the middle of a sentence. Go on after the Holy Spirit has stopped, and we are merely speaking out of our own mind. Attempt to prophecy when the Lord has not given us a word, and we speak only out of ourselves, something that is wholly human; attempt to operate a word of knowledge when God has not given revelation, and we are only guessing.

One of the very impressive things about the prophet Elisha is that he not only knew when God had revealed things to him, he also acknowledged when God had not done so. When the Shunammite woman whose son had died came and fell down and caught hold of the prophet's feet, Gehazi his servant went to push her away. Elisha said,

> '...Leave her alone! She is in bitter distress, but the Lord has hidden it from me and has not told me why.'
>
> (2 Kings 4:27)

Chapter 23

Conscience and the Will

Faith as the link or bridge between mind and spirit may be a new insight, but the link between conscience and the will is entirely familiar to us all. It is, of course, obedience. When conscience says, 'You ought', my will should respond, 'I will'. When conscience says 'You ought not', my will should say, 'I will not'.

There is no function of the human spirit more crucial to living out of the spirit than the conscience, but there are some aspects of obedience that need to be explored because they are so gravely misunderstood, even by mature Christians and many preachers.

For example, we sometimes give the impression that obedience is a kind of moral medicine. It is unpleasant so it must be good for us! At other times we confuse **obedience** with **conformity** – and conformity is one of the most dangerous features of modern society. It is one way people have of avoiding personal, moral responsibility. The responsibility of moral choices is delegated upwards to leaders, superiors, politicians, or the party machine. All the individual has to do is to obey orders, to do what he is told. The nature or consequences of those orders is no longer his concern.

This results in manifest evils taking place, for which nobody is responsible. The person who pulls the trigger or plants the bomb is not responsible: as a good soldier or a loyal subordinate he is merely obeying orders. The person who gives the orders hasn't killed anybody himself, nor spilled a drop of innocent blood; he feels no guilt. The chances are he is merely obeying orders himself, implementing a policy decision made even more bloodlessly further up still.

The Bible makes it quite clear that obedience merely as obedience is not of itself necessarily good.

> *Don't you know that when you offer yourselves to someone to obey him as slaves, you are slaves to the one whom you obey – whether you are slaves to sin, which leads to death, or to obedience which leads to righteousness?*   (Romans 6:16)

Love and freedom

Because of His nature and His purpose for humanity, God has committed Himself in a remarkable way to maintain each person's moral freedom. The response God seeks from His people is love and, as we have said elsewhere, love is a free moral choice, or it is nothing. The lover always has to take the risk that the one he loves may say 'no'. God took the risk that we would say 'no' to His love, and Calvary was the price He ultimately paid for that risk.

Because of His committal to the integrity of an individual's personhood, God has always limited His intervention in human affairs to the extent of human willingness. Even when the Father sent His Son into the world, it had to be through a yielded human will. When Gabriel came with the annunciation to Mary, nothing could happen until she uttered the marvelous words of submission,

> *'I am the Lord's servant ... May it be to me as you have said.'*   (Luke 1:38)

In the same way Christ, our redeemer, will not enter the heart until the will unbars the door. Once within the heart, He respects the human will just as much. The Holy Spirit, indwelling our recreated spirit, will not move out into the soul life without the free response of our will. Omnipotence will not crush even such a fragile thing as finite, feeble human will, so deeply is God committed to our moral being.

Love and obedience

▶ **Love expresses itself differently in different relationships.**

In the relationship of a person to God, or creature to Creator, or son to father, **love is primarily expressed in obedience.** Even in human terms, the love relationship of child to parent is *'Children obey your parents.'* (Note that we do not express love from parent to child as 'Parents obey your children.') Because it expresses love, the response from a person to God must be the freely given obedience of the heart. It must be more than bowing to superior force, or conformity on the basis of fear or pressure. For this reason the commands of God are given to the conscience and every person is always free to choose to obey or disobey.

> *But thanks be to God that, though you used to be slaves to sin, you wholeheartedly obeyed the form of teaching to which you were entrusted.* (Romans 6:17)

Because human beings are free to obey or disobey, the real nature of disobedience is also exposed. It is not weakness, nor misfortune, but rebellion, the refusal to love and the rejection of the Lover.

> *This is what the Lord says: 'Stand at the crossroads and look; ask for the ancient paths, ask where the good way is, and walk in it, and you will find rest for your souls.' But you said, 'We will not walk in it.'* (Jeremiah 6:16)

Obedience and freedom

One of the apparent paradoxes of the Christian life is that obedience makes us free. 'My will is not my own,' says the hymn writer, 'till I have made it thine.' He is right, and so are

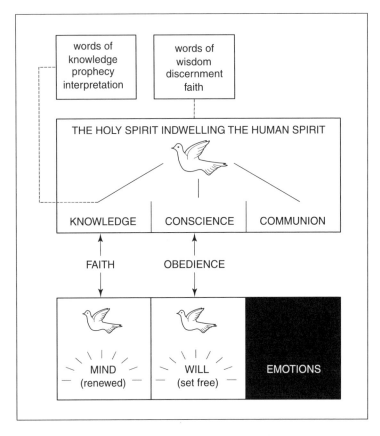

Figure 21: *Conscience and the will*

all the saints and mystics. Obedience and surrender, surprisingly, mean freedom and selfhood. Perhaps the diagram in Figure 21 will help us to understand how this happens.

Although God has a great interest in maintaining an individual's freedom, Satan has no such scruples. Human beings soon discovered that rebellion against obedient love to God did not secure freedom: it lost it. Into the power vacuum created by rebellion came Satan, and men and women found themselves in bondage to sin and snared in the tyranny of darkness. Even when, as Christians, we have been redeemed from the power of Satan, he still tries to ensnare our will. He utilizes the power of habit, and he plays on fears and desires – all in order to control and manipulate us. How then do we get free? There is only one way: that is by total obedience to the lordship of Jesus.

This aspect of lordship is generally overlooked. We major on our side of the relationship – obedience and committal, consecration and discipleship. But why does Jesus want to be Lord? Not so that he can 'lord it over' us. Not at all.

> *'You call me "Teacher" and "Lord", and rightly so, for this is what I am. Now that I, your Lord and Teacher, have washed your feet, you also should wash one another's feet.'*
>
> (John 13:13–14)

Jesus wants to be Lord so that He can carry out the responsibilities of lordship on our behalf.

▶ **He wants to be Lord because He is the only one wise enough to guide our lives properly, and the only one strong enough to keep us free from Satan.**

Under His lordship we know perfect freedom. But when we stray out from His protection our freedom won't last five minutes: the devil will see to that.

How does Jesus set us free today? In the same way that He set people free during His time on earth – by the power of the Holy Spirit.

> *'The Spirit of the Lord is on me, because he has anointed me to preach good news to the poor. He has sent me to proclaim freedom for the prisoners and recovery of sight for the blind, to release the oppressed ... '*
>
> (Luke 4:18)

When Jesus set people free from sickness, He did so by the anointing of the Holy Spirit (Acts 1:38); when He set them free from demons it was by the Spirit of God (Matthew 12:28). We are set free by that same Spirit. When we respond in obedience, the power of the Holy Spirit is released into the area of the human will.

> *...the Lord is the Spirit, and where the Spirit of the Lord is,*
> *there is freedom.*   (2 Corinthians 3:17)

Because He is the Spirit of liberty, everything He touches is
set free. Habits, compulsions, drug dependence, alcoholism
and inner bondage He cannot live with; therefore, He breaks
the yoke and sets us at liberty. There is nothing on this earth
to be compared with being free to delight in doing the will of
God.

> *It is for freedom that Christ has set us free.*   (Galatians 5:1)

Obedience and ability

We can now begin to see how God's commands are also His
enabling. When we respond with our weak human obedience
to His commands, the power of the Holy Spirit can reach
across into our human will so that the weakest-willed
Christian can *'do everything through him who gives me strength'*
(Philippians 4:13).

We read the commands of God, *'Be holy because I am holy'*, or
'Love your enemies, and pray for those who persecute you,' and we
cry 'Impossible!' But God does not lower His standards because
human beings have failed. Instead, He indwells a person by
His Holy Spirit; and when that person responds in obedience,
the Spirit comes alongside the weak human will and lifts it
into the ability to fulfill the righteousness of the law.

> *...in order that the righteous requirements of the law might*
> *be fully met in us, who do not live according to the sinful*
> *nature but according to the Spirit.*   (Romans 8:4)

> *...for it is God who works in you to will and to act according*
> *to his good purpose.*   (Philippians 2:13)

This is God's way of enabling. Through obedience we can
discover for ourselves that His grace is sufficient for us, too:

> *...for my power is made perfect in weakness.*
>   (2 Corinthians 12:9)

Obedience and knowledge

As we have said, the relationship of conscience and will is crucial in the whole matter of walking in the Spirit. Not only is the power to do the will of God available only through obedience, but obedience is critical in knowing the voice of God. Disobedience, because it shuts out the Holy Spirit from the soul life, is an insuperable barrier to hearing from God. I find it very difficult to hear the voice of God – not because God is not speaking, but because I do not really want to hear, in case He wants me to talk about my disobedience! I may say I want to hear God speak, but actually I want to be selective in what I hear. And that just does not work.

That is why guidance is so difficult if we are disobedient, or there is something troubling our conscience. I am not suggesting that all problems in guidance stem from disobedience or unconfessed sin. By no means! What I am saying is that disobedience or unconfessed sin **always** creates problems with guidance.

It is the same with spiritual understanding. Jesus made it clear that obedience is the way to the knowledge of God.

> *If anyone chooses to do God's will, he will find out whether my teaching comes from God or whether I speak on my own.*
> (John 7:17)

Now we can begin to see how God created us so that we could live in responsive obedience to divine wisdom without negating or ignoring the God-given faculties of reason and human judgment.

In the ordinary situations we face every day, we receive information from the circumstances and factors that are involved. Our mind and our feelings work on this data, analyzing, evaluating and judging. But through our spirit we have access to data from another source: we have information from God's standpoint, the way things look in the light of divine wisdom. When we need to make a better decision than is possible from temporal data, or when sensory knowledge would lead us astray, divine wisdom reaches us by the witness of the Spirit to our conscience.

216 of the Spirit

Sometimes there may come a check to our conscience even though the prudent course of action we should take seems clear enough to our mind. To which source of direction does the will then pay heed: the mind or the conscience, external circumstance or the voice of the Spirit? Here is how Jesus handled such situations.

> *By myself I can do nothing; I judge only as I hear, and my judgment is just, for I seek not to please myself but him who sent me.*   (John 5:30)

Ultimately Jesus decided not on sense evidence, but by what He 'heard' in His spirit: that is, in His conscience. His judgment was always right: because His obedience was perfect, therefore His 'hearing' was unimpaired. How would you like to be always right in your judgments? Certainly we will never match the judgment of Jesus – not because we do not have access to the same wisdom, for He Himself is now made wisdom to us – but because our obedience is imperfect and partial. But the Holy Spirit understands all this and He still wants and is able to guide us, given only our willingness to obey.

There is a very interesting illustration in the sixteenth chapter of Acts. It is clear that Paul was trying to find the guidance of the Spirit in much the same way as we often do: by trial and error!

In verse 6 we read that,

> *Paul and his companions traveled throughout the region of Phrygia and Galatia, having been kept by the Holy Spirit from preaching the word in the province of Asia.*

Was Paul responding to a 'check', a sense of hesitation in his spirit? Kept from preaching the word in Asia. Why? No reason from circumstances, and no immediate direction, so they try elsewhere.

Verse 7:

> *When they came to the border of Mysia, they tried to enter Bithynia, but the Spirit of Jesus would not allow them to.*

Again there is no witness of the Holy Spirit's assent to their plans, perhaps even an inward sense of being stopped, so they withdraw from their plans.

But when they come to Troas, Paul has a vision of a man from Macedonia saying, *'Come over to Macedonia and help us.'*

> *After Paul had seen the vision, we got ready at once to leave for Macedonia, concluding that God had called us to preach the gospel to them.*   (Acts 16:10)

They were right. But had they not been obedient to the earlier checks of the Spirit, they would not have been in the position to receive and recognize the guidance of God when it came.

Concerning spiritual gifts

Word of wisdom

What we have been studying also has relevance to the operation of particular spiritual gifts. For example, what Paul experienced in a vision in Acts 16 was **a word of wisdom** (1 Corinthians 12:8). Wisdom, as we pointed out earlier, is related to the attainment of goals. It is directive and, because it is directive, calls for obedience.

One test of the reliability of a word of wisdom, is the extent to which the person through whom it comes is living a life of real and humble obedience himself.

▶   **If you are not obedient to the will of God for your own life you will be unlikely to know the will of God for someone else's life.**

The word of wisdom is a gift exercised by the mature – not those who have not yet themselves been tested in the school of obedience. An understanding of this would avoid many problems and much heartache from directive prophecy given by those who are new and untried in the realm of spiritual gifts. Certainly there is a prophetic ministry that is directive and can disclose the will of God for our lives, but it is a ministry of maturity. There are not many prophets in the Church today, and the genuine ones are people who themselves have been through the crucible of God. For the rest, the Lord's reply to those who ask, *'Lord, what about him?'* is, *'What is that to you? You must follow me'* (John 21:22).

Discernment of spirits

Another spiritual gift that bears directly on the function of conscience is the **discernment of spirits** (1 Corinthians 12:10). In our earlier discussion of the role of the conscience, we pointed out that it bore witness to truth. It is conscience that bears witness to the truth or falsehood of a spirit, human or otherwise.

It is impossible to over-emphasize the importance of a clean conscience in the ministry of deliverance, because the presence of an evil spirit is ultimately known by discernment not by symptoms. I have been faced with manifestations that had all the hallmarks of a classic case of demon-possession, only to find that they were the result of deep emotional hurt or mental stress. On the other hand, I have gone to pray for someone with a physical need and found a demonic cause. Discernment is knowing the truth about a spiritual situation; and because it is the conscience that bears witness to truth, accurate discernment needs a clean conscience.

A similar situation applies in the judging of prophecy; in fact, in 1 Corinthians 12, discernment is linked to prophecy in almost the same way as interpretation is linked with tongues. A prophecy may come from one of three sources. It may come from the Holy Spirit, it may come merely from the human spirit of the person who prophesies, or – more rarely – it may come from a deceiving spirit. How then are we to decide whether a word of prophecy is really from the Lord or not? 1 John 4:2–3 says:

> *This is how you can recognize the Spirit of God: Every spirit that acknowledges that Jesus Christ has come in the flesh is from God, but every spirit that does not acknowledge Jesus is not from God...*

This is a vital test, but it is not much help in the most common situation we face; that is, in deciding whether the prophecy that somebody brings forth in tonight's meeting is really the Lord speaking. Perhaps it is just something from his own spirit that he thought was from the Lord. The answer is found in 1 John 4:6:

> *We are from God, and whoever knows God listens to us; but whoever is not from God does not listen to us. This is how we recognize the Spirit of truth and the spirit of falsehood.*

In John's gospel and epistles, terms such as seeing and hearing refer most often to spiritual seeing or hearing. *'Listen'* is used in this way here. John says that a true spiritual utterance is one that the people of God 'hear' not just with their ears but in their spirit. Therefore, if you want to know whether a prophecy was from the Lord or not, and you are not sure whether you heard it in your own conscience, ask around. Find out if other spiritual people in the meeting 'heard' it or not. Just as the operation of the gift of prophecy is strongly intuitive, judging prophecy is similarly intuitive.

There is one further aspect of judging prophecy that is very important. The more our conscience is exposed to the input of the Scriptures (the *'more certain'* word of prophecy as Peter calls it), the more will our spiritual senses be exercised to discern the true from the false, the divine from the human, when we hear it spoken in a meeting.

Faith

Finally there is the spiritual gift of **faith** (1 Corinthians 12:9). We mention it in this context because faith always requires a response from the will as well as the mind. If it never gets beyond mere intellectual assent it will never affect our behavior and it will never amount to Bible faith. Believing in the Scriptures always has a strong volitional element; therefore trusting and obeying always go together.

> *By faith Abraham, when called to go to a place he would later receive as his inheritance, obeyed and went . . .*
>
> (Hebrews 11:8)

The saga of the Old Testament saints who had the gift of faith is a chronicle of those who acted on that faith: Noah building the ark, Abraham offering up Isaac, Moses passing through the Red Sea, Gideon with his three hundred men, David with his sling against Goliath. So, if we are asking for the gift of faith, let it be on the clear understanding that it will demand obedience, the kind Peter displayed at the temple gate.

'... Silver or gold I do not have, but what I have I give you. In the name of Jesus Christ of Nazareth, walk.' Taking him by the right hand, he helped him up, and instantly the man's feet and ankles became strong.   (Acts 3:6–7)

Chapter 24

Worship and the Emotions

We have discovered that living out of our spirit means that the spirit's intuitive faculty takes precedence over the reasoning of the mind, and that conscience directs the will. We now have to see how the function of worship or communion belonging to the spirit is meant to govern the emotional reactions of the soul.

This is certainly unfamiliar territory. Like me, you have probably assumed that any control over the emotions must come from the will. We say to a person, 'Control your temper' or 'Don't let yourself get upset'. But this kind of control is of very limited effectiveness; and, in any case, it appears to work only one way. That is to say, feelings may be suppressed by the will, but they cannot so easily be produced by willpower. I cannot will myself to be happy, or sad, or even fearful. The harder I try, the more impossible it becomes to produce any emotional response at all.

God created human beings in His image, in such a way that the governing center of an individual's personality was intended to be not the will but the human spirit. Furthermore, a Christian has access through his spirit to the person of the indwelling Holy Spirit. But what relevance does this have as far as the emotional life is concerned? There is obviously some significance, because the Holy Spirit clearly possesses all the qualities that we most want in our emotional life: love, joy, peace, patience, kindness, goodness, faithfulness and self-control (Galatians 5:22–23). The question is: 'How do we give the Holy Spirit, dwelling in our spirit, access into the area of

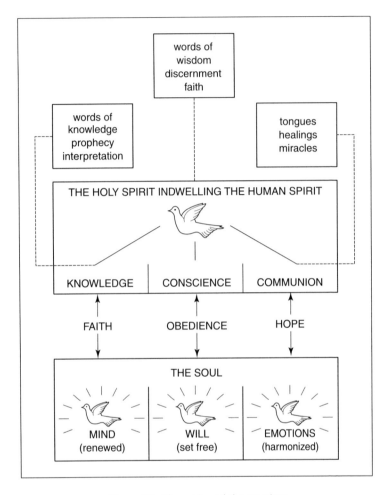

Figure 22: *The spirit and the emotions*

our feelings?' What is the bridge that links worship with the area of the soul-life in which we experience feelings?

It is a critical question because the place where people are hurting most is in the realm of their emotions. The answer can be summed up in one word, at once the most neglected and the most misunderstood word in all Scripture. You can see it in Figure 22. It is: **hope**.

Hope – the neglected virtue

Paul concludes his wonderful hymn to love in 1 Corinthians with the well-known words:

> *And now these three remain: faith, hope and love. But the greatest of these is love.* (1 Corinthians 13:13)

In 1 Thessalonians he links the three again:

> *We continually remember before our God and Father your work produced by faith, your labor prompted by love, and your endurance inspired by hope in our Lord Jesus Christ.* (1 Thessalonians 1:3)

Yet here is a very strange thing. In my time I have listened to hundreds of sermons on the theme of faith, and probably as many on love. As far as I can remember, in all my life I have heard only two sermons on hope – and I preached them both myself. True, Paul says that love is the greatest; but if hope is only third it should not have been so sadly neglected. Perhaps the sound of the word in English has something to do with it. Hope sounds somehow weak and tentative. 'I only hope I can.' 'There isn't much hope really.' But Paul was right. Hope is a wonderful and life-changing concept – when we understand what it really means.

Let me give a definition of Bible hope. Learn it by heart.

▶   **Hope is the confident expectation of something good.**

Note that this definition of hope has three basic roots:

1.   Confidence
2.   Expectancy
3.   Security

Hope, because it is confident, secure and expectant, creates in the person who has it an inner attitude of openness towards God, openness towards other people, and openness towards life. This is of extreme importance, because we will experience only what we receive, and we will receive only what we are open to.

Openness to receive is comparatively rare, even among Christians. There are two main classes of people. The first say, 'Never expect anything and then you won't be disappointed.' They are the optimists. The pessimists say, 'Always expect the worst, then you won't be disappointed whatever happens.' Do you think I'm being unfair? Then consider how many of us habitually maintain protective barricades against life, against people and against God – then wonder why we never seem to receive anything!

Hope is really the other side of faith. Faith means that I commit myself in trust to another. Hope means that I expect that what I have offered will be responded to, therefore I am open to receive that response. Out of that trust and expectation the possibility for love arises. It takes faith and hope to create love. We could legitimately put 1 Corinthians 13:13 in the form of a Pauline equation:

Faith + Hope = Love

Many attempts at personal relationships are stillborn, either because we are afraid to commit ourselves in trust to the other person, or because we have no confidence that what we have offered the other is of value and will be appreciated and responded to. We fail to bridge the gap between us: either we do not reach the other person, or we do not allow him to reach us.

A shy person – or one with an inferiority complex – has a problem with hope. I can remember saying to myself in my younger days, 'Never let people get close to you, because if they ever find out what you are like they will immediately lose interest.' So I never took the risk.

Many people have the same problem with God. Not so much an unwillingness to trust themselves to God, but the lack of any clear assurance that God values what they offer Him, and will respond in any way to their overtures. Sometimes I ask such people 'If, right now, you were to ask God for something, do you really think that He would hear you and answer you?' Most times they look wistful and say, 'I wish I could believe it, but to be honest I don't feel that God is really interested in me.'

Exactly the reverse is true. To the Father we, as individuals, are of inestimable value. He tells us that we are bought with a great price and that the very hairs of our head are all numbered. Therefore, when we reach out in trust, or in worship, or in need to God, He always, always responds. That is why a confident expectancy of good things from God is always well founded.

> *And hope does not disappoint us, because God has poured out his love into our hearts by the Holy Spirit, whom he has given us.* (Romans 5:5)

The constant attitude of confident expectancy should be the hallmark of every believer, because our God is the God of hope.

> *May the God of hope fill you with all joy and peace as you trust in him, so that you may overflow with hope by the power of the Holy Spirit.* · (Romans 15:13)

Hope and the mind

I must confess that for a long time I have a very little real understanding about the full armor of God in Ephesians 6. I could imagine the various pieces of hardware (and mentally picture myself struggling into them like a medieval knight), but it seemed to have very little practical significance. Then one day, as I was reading 1 Thessalonians 5:8, I saw something:

> *But since we belong to the day, let us be self-controlled, putting on faith and love as a breastplate, and the hope of salvation as a helmet.*

There they were – faith, hope and love again – but now I realized that **hope is meant to be the guardian of the**

mind, the perfect protection against depression, worry, pessimism and all forms of negative thinking. Where, after all, do these evil things breed? In a mind that is shut up in the dark with only its fears for company. What drives out the dark? Light. How do you let the light in? Open up. What drives out fear? Perfect love. How do you get love? Faith and hope, trust and expectancy, courage to give and openness to receive!

Abraham was a classic exponent of this kind of hope.

> *Against all hope, Abraham in hope believed and so became the father of many nations, just as it had been said to him . . .*   (Romans 4:18)

But Jesus himself was the supreme man of hope. There never ever was before – or since – a life of hope like that. The sharing of the bread and the cup at supper – that touching expression of love and reconciliation – was not an empty gesture. I believe that in His blessed humanity Jesus hoped right up to the end that Judas would draw back and save himself. Jesus also knew Peter's fatal flaw. He knew that Peter would break and deny Him, but still He said:

> *'Simon, Simon, Satan has asked to sift you as wheat. But I have prayed for you, Simon, that your faith may not fail. And when you have turned back, strengthen your brothers.'*
> (Luke 22:31–32)

Hope and the emotions

Primarily, however, we need to see the place of hope as far as the emotions are concerned. Take David in Psalm 42, in one of his bleaker moods with which we can easily identify.

> *'Why are you downcast, O my soul?*
> *Why so disturbed within me?'*   (Psalm 42:5a)

But David knew the great therapeutic value of hope for disturbed feelings. He cries,

'Put your hope in God,
for I will yet praise him,
my Savior and my God.'   (Psalm 42:5b)

The attitude of openness and expectancy that the Bible calls hope is vitally important for our emotional balance. It is not just blind optimism or 'what will be, will be' fatalism. Hope is a confident, open attitude towards God, because we know that all His choices for us are motivated by infinite love and guided by infinite wisdom. Every good and perfect gift, we learn, comes from our Father who is totally unvarying in His goodness (James 1:17). In the most difficult and trying circumstances we discover that God is working for our good (Romans 8:28). Who would not be open to receive on such terms?

Often we perceive situations as threatening or beyond our capacity to manage, and so we react defensively in fear, or anger, or irritation. But when we have an attitude of openness towards God, we respond also to data from another source, we see situations and circumstances from a place of inner security, we measure difficulties and problems against the ability of God who is for us and on our side.

There is a beautiful example in the Old Testament. Elisha is in Dothan and the city becomes surrounded by Syrian armies. The prophet's servant is panic-stricken. *'Oh, my lord, what shall we do?'* But Elisha, strangely, is unafraid. He is calm because he has other information to go on.

'Don't be afraid ... Those who are with us are more than those who are with them.'
And Elisha prayed, 'O Lord, open his eyes so that he may see.' Then the LORD *opened the servant's eyes, and he looked and saw the hills full of horses and chariots of fire all round Elisha.*   (2 Kings 6:16–17)

Hope is, however, of far greater importance than merely giving us truer and more reliable information to guide our emotional responses. As you saw in Figure 22, it provides the essential link that is needed to allow the Holy Spirit to come across into the area of our feelings.

We have already explored the significance of this in terms of emotional healing, but it bears brief repetition here also.

Firstly, it gives the Holy Spirit access to cleanse and heal the hurts that often lie buried in our feelings: experiences of rejection, resentment, grief, failure and so on. It is the expectant, trusting openness of hope that allows the Holy Spirit into the emotions to deal with buried needs. When we allow Him to do so we will marvel at the infinite skill and the tender compassion with which He works.

Secondly, it enables the Holy Spirit to remove emotional hang-ups that may have inhibited growth in this area of our personality. We are, Paul says in Ephesians 4:15, *'in all things to grow up into him who is the Head, that is, Christ.'* Many Christians are spiritually and mentally mature, but emotionally immature.

What is the answer? We cannot be forgiven for being immature, we cannot even be healed from it. We can only grow out of it. The Holy Spirit is the Spirit of adoption (Romans 8:15), the Spirit who brings us to maturity as sons and daughters. He can remove the blockage, whatever it is: a fear of failure, an inferiority complex, a negative self-image, or an in-built sense of worthlessness. I have seen all these, and many more, taken away by the Holy Spirit – and people set free to grow up into beautiful emotional maturity.

Thirdly – and this is very exciting – the attitude of expectant welcome that characterizes hope allows the Holy Spirit to express His nature in us.

▶ **This is how the fruits of the Holy Spirit are grafted into our nature.**

I often wondered how such a thing was meant to happen. Preaching I heard suggested that, in some way, we had to copy or imitate the Holy Spirit. How can you imitate feelings without being totally insincere? Does obedience produce the fruits? Or is it faith? In fact, it is hope that does it.

Openness is the key. The fruits of the Holy Spirit are meant to be experienced in our feelings, firstly because they are themselves feelings, and secondly because feelings are the most powerful motivators of behavior. There is, indeed, a most beautiful balance in all this.

1. God shares His **truth** with us. It is received by **spiritual intuition** and illuminates the **mind**.
2. God shares His **wisdom** with us. It is discerned by the **conscience** and responded to by the **will**.
3. God shares His **love** with us. It is experienced in **worship** and felt in the **emotions**.

From this divine sharing of Himself we are to know not only what it is to have the mind of Christ (1 Corinthians 2:16), and to experience God working in us to will and to act (Philippians 2:13), but also to feel the affections of Christ.

> *God can testify how I long for all of you with the affection of Christ Jesus.* (Philippians 1:8)

We are meant to feel in our hearts the flow of Christ's unchanging, unconditional love for others. There are times when I have known this, but always it is given; that is to say, we cannot work it up or produce it out of ourselves. We cannot even imagine what it is like before it happens, because the love of God is qualitatively different from human love. But God has so much of it that He wills out of His fullness to pour out His love in our hearts by the Holy Spirit. Our only contribution – if it can be called that – is the openness and expectancy that enables us to receive what is given.

Concerning spiritual gifts

Tongues

What we have been considering so far may also illuminate some misunderstood aspects of the spiritual gifts, particularly the gift of **tongues**. We deal with tongues here because it is first and foremost a matter of communication and, as we have already pointed out, communication is something we do with our spirit.

I communicate with another person only when I reach out in my spirit and touch his spirit. It is possible, therefore, to have a real meeting and genuine communication without using words at all. We can meet, reach out in love and empathy to one another, smile or embrace, and not speak a word. In times of deep emotion (for example love, grief or sympathy), that is often what happens. But if in a twenty-year friendship we never ever spoke words to one another, it would be a very limited sort of relationship.

How then, are we to understand the essential nature of an experience like the baptism in the Holy Spirit? The baptism in the Spirit is not tongues, nor is it joy, nor peace, nor power, nor holiness. Any or all of these may accompany it, but it in itself is none of these things.

▶ **The baptism in the Holy Spirit is essentially the meeting of two persons: one person is God the Holy Spirit, the other is our human spirit.**

It is perfectly true that in this experience, when my spirit meets the Holy Spirit, tongues are not necessary. There can be a genuine meeting and real communication without tongues. But when my spirit meets the blessed Holy Spirit Himself, my spirit has things to say, things to express for which the mind cannot find adequate utterance. Speaking in tongues is the wonderful gift of the Holy Spirit that provides the spirit with its own medium of communication.

> *For if I pray in a tongue, my spirit prays . . .*
>   (1 Corinthians 14:14)

> *For anyone who speaks in a tongue does not speak to men but to God . . . he utters mysteries with his spirit.*
>   (1 Corinthians 14:2)

The best theological description of tongues I have ever heard came from a friend of mind who was converted and filled with the Holy Spirit when he was a crane driver on the Wellington wharves. He described tongues as:

'a spiritual overdrive that goes straight from our spirit to the Holy Spirit, without being clogged up by the gearbox of our mind.'

That's nearly perfect!

When we understand that tongues are nothing more or less than a communications medium, we will also see that it is not necessary that their use is accompanied by a great feeling of excitement. Sometimes when I speak English I get very excited. Most times however, I am very matter of fact. Sometimes when I pray in tongues I am stirred or exalted, but at other times my spirit just has plain ordinary things to say to God.

Healings and miracles

The gift of **healings** and the gift of **miracles** can be considered in the same context as tongues, because with them also, the element of communication is central, even though it is communication of power, not of words. There is a fundamental identity in the Scripture between word and power. Healing power followed the words of Jesus; His word had power over demons; the Lord worked with the apostles confirming His word by the signs that followed, and so on.

In the operation of the gifts of healings and miracles there must be an attitude of openness in two directions:

1.   A reaching out in confident expectancy to the Holy Spirit who heals or performs the miracles.
2.   An openness towards the one to whom we are ministering, so that what we receive from the Lord we give to them.

The gift of healings is not praying for the sick to be healed – it is healing them. We are commanded to **preach** the kingdom, but to **heal** the sick (Matthew 10:7–8). Therefore, the gift of healings can operate independently of faith on the part of the sick person, but because of this we need to know the mind of the Lord for a particular situation.

The healing of the lame man at the temple gate is a case in point. The apostles, perhaps Jesus Himself, had probably passed him by many times before, for it seems to have been his regular begging place. But this time Peter senses in his spirit something different. To the lame man who, as far as we can tell, was not even thinking about being healed, he says,

> *'Look at us . . . Silver or gold I do not have, but what I have I give you. In the name of Jesus Christ of Nazareth, walk.'*
>
> (Acts 3:6)

With this inner attitude of openness there is, inevitably, an emotional involvement with the needs that are to be met. Jesus, as He saw the needy throngs, was moved with compassion towards them. I greatly doubt whether a healing ministry is possible without a heart that is moved with compassion. Indeed, a compassionate heart may well be the beginning of a healing ministry.

Chapter 25

The Word Made Flesh

We have been studying the various responses that are necessary for the power of the Holy Spirit to be released from our spirit into the areas of the mind, the emotions and the will. We have to take this one stage further. The purpose of God in creating human beings like Himself, was to share the realities of the spiritual realm with the realm of nature. Therefore, the power of the Spirit is meant to affect not only our soul-life, but also our body-life.

I first linked this with the question of healing; but more than healing is involved: it is the whole process of the Word becoming flesh in us. We will begin, however, with physical healing.

Because the Holy Spirit is the Spirit of life (Romans 8:2), everything He touches must live; indeed we are specifically told in Romans 8:11 that He will give life to our mortal bodies. The question I faced was this. If I am sick, how do I release the power of the Holy Spirit, not only into my soul, but also into my body in order that He can heal it? There must be some necessary response on my part, for the Spirit will no more force His way into the body without the free consent of my will than He will into the soul.

The principles I discovered are set out in Figure 23. Remember that they are relevant not only to healing, but to the whole question of living out of the spirit.

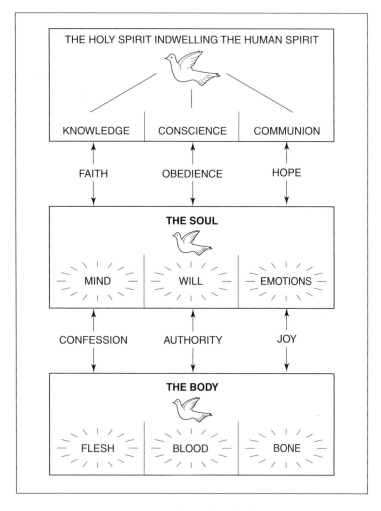

Figure 23: *The Word made flesh*

Faith and confession

Christians, particularly those with an evangelical background, find it hard to accept that in the context of
redemption, the Bible hardly ever speaks of faith on its
own. For example:

- In **salvation, repentance** is combined with faith.

  ... turn to God in repentance and have faith in our Lord Jesus Christ. (Acts 20:21)

- In **sanctification, obedience** is combined with faith.

  ... chosen according to the foreknowledge of God the Father, through the sanctifying work of the Spirit, for obedience to Jesus Christ and sprinkling by his blood.
  (1 Peter 1:2)

  God chose you to be saved through the sanctifying work of the Spirit and through belief in the truth.
  (2 Thessalonians 2:13)

- In **healing, confession** is combined with faith.

Sickness is, of course, a complex problem. The factors that are involved do not fall into one simple, universal pattern. Any attempt, therefore, to apply one uniform approach to every case of healing is bound to cause difficulties. Jesus never did – which is why we sometimes find it hard to understand why, in particular instances, He said or did the things He did. We cannot open up here the whole subject of healing. My own conviction is that the miracles of Jesus, properly understood, give us the keys to every possible class of circumstances we are likely to meet in the ministry of healing.

Where faith is the essential key to healing – as it often is – the other, and often neglected, component is confession. The word *'homologeo'* means literally 'to speak the same thing'.

▶ **Confession means that, out of a deep conviction of the truth of what God says, I speak out my assent or agreement with His word.**

The classic exposition of confession is in the tenth chapter of Romans.

> *... 'The word is near you; it is in your mouth and in your heart', that is, the word of faith we are proclaiming: That if you confess with your mouth, 'Jesus is Lord', and believe in*

your heart that God raised him from the dead, you will be saved. For it is with your heart that you believe and are justified, and it is with your mouth that you confess and are saved.   (Romans 10:8–10)

The Greek word used here for 'salvation' is *'sozo'*, which also means 'to be healed or to be made whole'. Therefore, this passage says that to be healed I need two things: a heart to believe (resulting in righteousness, a right relationship with God), and a mouth to confess (resulting in healing).

Another basic meaning of righteousness in the Bible is 'conformity to what is normal'. God is righteous because God is always perfectly what God ought to be. In the book of Job, it says that God gave a man back his righteousness. It means God healed him. Health, not sickness, is the normal state that God ordained for human beings. So:

▶   **faith in the heart restores what is normal, which is health; and confession with the mouth brings it to pass.**

Many times we do not receive the results of our faith because we do not confess it with our mouth. The provision that God has made to meet our need remains real, but only potential – it never becomes actual.

Scripture places a great deal of emphasis on confession.

'I tell you the truth, if anyone says to this mountain, "Go, throw yourself into the sea," and does not doubt in his heart but believes that what he says will happen, it will be done for him.'   (Mark 11:23)

It is written, 'I believed; therefore I have spoken.' With that same spirit of faith we also believe and therefore speak...
                                                   (2 Corinthians 4:13)

Jesus spoke the word of faith, when He said to Jairus, *'The child is not dead but asleep'* (Mark 5:39); to the blind man, *'Receive your sight; your faith has healed you'* (Luke 18:42); and before the tomb of Lazarus, *'Father, I thank you that you have heard me ... Lazarus, come out!'* (John 11:41, 43).

What is the reason for this emphasis on speaking? It is more than the public confession of private faith, although that is an element. It is a far greater principle that, if we grasp it, can revolutionize our whole faith-life.

First, consider the way in which God creates. God, the uncreated Creator, made everything that He created by means of His word: He spoke it into existence.

> *Now the earth was formless and empty, darkness was over the surface of the deep, and the Spirit of God was hovering over the waters. And God said, 'Let there be light', and there was light.* (Genesis 1:2–3)

Out of His Spirit, God spoke the creative word and all the wonders of creation sprang into being.

> *By faith we understand that the universe was formed at God's command, so that what was seen was not made out of what was visible.* (Hebrews 11:3)

Secondly, human beings, made in the image of God, are created creators. Animals are locked into the pattern of behavior that ensures their adaptation to the environment. We call it instinct. But people are different from animals. We can select our own behavior and choose our own goals. In other words, we can create.

How do human beings create? We create in the same way as God created.

▶ **We create out of our human spirits by speaking things into existence.**

What we conceive in the spirit we express. We communicate, and speak into existence things either good or bad.

> *For out of the overflow of the heart the mouth speaks. The good man brings good things out of the good stored up in*

> *him, and the evil man brings evil things out of the evil stored*
> *up in him.*   (Matthew 12:34–35)

If we ask how wickedness has become so rampant in
society, the answer is that human beings spoke it into
existence. How did the permissive society happen? It was
spoken into being. Do you see why it is in Satan's interest to
control the media? He knows this principle. Can you understand why he strives to keep the mouths of Christians closed?
So that they will not create. True, we witness by what we are,
as well as by what we say, but there is one fatal flaw in a
witness that is only of life and not of words: such a life rarely
creates, seldom reproduces itself. Underline this basic truth
until it is etched into your entire being:

> ▶ **Human beings create by speaking into being what is**
>   **in our spirits.**

When we speak the word of faith, we speak God's will and
God's provision into being. The promises that God makes,
to meet our needs, constitute real but still only potential
provision. It is like money credited to our account in the
bank. It is real wealth but only potential. It will not pay our
bills, it will not purchase a loaf of bread or a bottle of milk,
just by staying in the bank. We can die of starvation or be
jailed for not paying our bills, and the money can be there
against our name all the time.

It is the same with the promises of God. Faith reaches out
and receives the provision; confession speaks it into actual
material fact. Faith, to revert to our illustration, is writing the
check; confession is handing the check across the counter in
exchange for goods.

An experience of healing illuminated this very vividly for
me. I had, at one time, an infection of the inner ear that
upsets the sense of balance so that I had repeated dizzy spells.
It got better after a time, but the doctor said there was no
guarantee, in view of my age, that it would not recur. One
Monday morning, months later, I got up and went into the
bathroom, only to have the walls begin to perform tight

circles around my head. At the time I was running a series of seminars on healing.

My first thought in the bathroom that morning was 'I won't be able to go to the seminar tonight.' My second thought was, 'How do I explain why I can't go to the seminar tonight?' My third thought was more positive. I reached out in my faith and got in contact with the Lord, and received in my faith the healing I needed. Then I began to confess what the Lord has said in Isaiah 53, 'By his wounds we are healed … by his wounds I am healed.'

I hung on to that confession all morning. At first I had to be careful because if I turned my head too quickly the world began to spin; but by midday I was healed – and the trouble has never recurred. The healing was there in the Holy Spirit all the time, because He is the Spirit of life. Faith reached out and received the provision, so that His power could enter the area of my mind; confession spoke it into being so that His power could enter my body. The result in my body had to be divine order and divine wholeness: literally, divine balance!

Both faith and confession are necessary. If the faith link is not there, all you have is mind over matter; you have the power of positive thinking. But that is not what we are talking about. You cannot speak into existence what you have not received in your faith. Faith rests on the certainty of revelation knowledge. It 'sees' what has been provided and reaches out to receive it. Then faith uses the creative word to speak into existence what has been received.

Obedience and authority

Elsewhere we have explored various aspects of the relationship between obedience and authority, but the one that concerns us here is authority as the outworking of obedience.

To begin with, we must understand that it has always been part of God's plan that human beings should exercise authority.

> *Then God said, 'Let us make man in our image, in our likeness, and let them rule over the fish of the sea and the birds of the*

*air, over the livestock, over all the earth, and over all the
creatures that move along the ground.'*   (Genesis 1:26)

God has never changed His mind about that, in spite of
human rebellion. It is true that atonement and redemption
became necessary because of sin; but when He has completed
His work, God will end up with exactly what He set out to
achieve: human beings in His own image and according
to His own likeness, having rule over creation.

Because authority is the exercise of delegated power, it can
be exercised only by those who are in an obedient relationship to the source of that power. God's power is not a
substance separate from Himself that He can hand over to
someone else. Power (*dunamis*) belongs to the nature and
being of God, and only God can use it. It moves only at His
volition. But God wills to exercise His power through
redeemed human beings so that we have the privilege of
sharing in the divine initiative. We can do so only when we
are in a relationship of loving obedience towards God so that
we know, in any particular situation, firstly **what** God wants
to do about it, and secondly, **when** He wants to do it.

The Roman centurion who so impressed Jesus with his
faith understood this principle perfectly:

> *'But say the word and my servant will be healed. For I myself
> am a man under authority, with soldiers under me. I tell this
> one, "Go," and he goes; and that one, "Come," and he
> comes. I say to my servant, "Do this," and he does it.'*
>
> (Luke 7:7–8)

Notice that the centurion did not say he was a man with
authority: he said he was a man under authority. Only
because he was under authority did he have authority. His
men obeyed his orders without question – not because he
was personally stronger than any of them, but because they
knew that the power of the centurion's superiors was behind
his orders, and theirs behind them, all the way back to Caesar
in Rome. Provided the centurion stayed under authority, he
had behind him all the power of the Roman State.

Do you see what this means as far as the Christian is concerned? It means that, in facing situations of need or difficulty, we do not need to possess any resources of power within ourselves. All we need is to remain in a position of obedience to the lordship of Jesus Christ, and all the power of the kingdom of God will back us up.

The purpose of obedience is therefore to enable God to entrust us with authority. The whole thrust of the parable of the talents in Luke 19 lies right there. The nobleman was not concerned with making money out of slaves, but with making rulers out of servants. He was investing not in cash, but in lives. Therefore to those who had responded in obedience he said, *'Because you have been trustworthy in a very small matter, take charge of ten cities'* (Luke 19:17).

Authority is strictly proportional to obedience: ten talents, ten cities, five talents, five cities, and so on. God's purpose is to take those who have been slaves to sin and Satan, and to teach them the free, loving response to His will that is obedience from the heart, so that they can be entrusted with the exercise of rule and authority. Therefore, obedience must precede authority.

In Jesus we see obedience to the will and purpose of the Father that was absolute. Therefore, the authority He exercised was also absolute. It marked His whole life and ministry. 'The man with authority' was one of the designations by which He was known. Look at these examples:

- **Teaching**

  . . . he taught as one who had authority . . .
  (Matthew 7:29)

- **Healing**

  . . . they were filled with awe; and they praised God, who had given such authority to men.   (Matthew 9:8)

- **Exorcism**

  . . . with authority! He even gives orders to evil spirits and they obey him.   (Mark 1:27)

- **Over nature**

  ... 'Who is this? He commands even the winds and the water, and they obey him.'   (Luke 8:25)

- **Over sin**

  '... the Son of Man has authority on earth to forgive sins.'   (Luke 5:24)

- **Over life and death**

  '... I lay down my life – only to take it up again ... I have authority to lay it down and authority to take it up again.'   (John 10: 17–18)

Finally, by virtue of His death and resurrection, Jesus has **all authority**!

> *Then Jesus came to them and said, 'All authority in heaven and on earth has been given to me.'*   (Matthew 28:18)

Christ has not only delegated authority to the Church but, in the person of the indwelling Holy Spirit, He has provided the power (*dunamis*) to back up that authority. When, in His humanity, Jesus spoke the word of authority, it was the power of the Holy Spirit within Him that enforced the command.

> *'But if I drive out demons by the Spirit of God, then the kingdom of God has come upon you.'*   (Matthew 12:28)

> *God anointed Jesus of Nazareth with the Holy Spirit and power, and ... he went around doing good and healing all who were under the power of the devil, because God was with him.*   (Acts 10:38)

Thus, when Jesus told the disciples about the baptism in the Holy Spirit, He could assure them from His own experience that they, too, would receive access to power, or *dunamis*, just as He had. We are not required to bring to bear any resources of power to meet needs, or overcome the devil, or set people free. The Holy Spirit within us has all power at

His disposal. Our responsibility is to allow the Holy Spirit access to the situation.

The authority conferred on the believer therefore depends on two factors: one is the power and authority that belongs to Christ as Head of the Church; the other is our relationship to Him as risen Lord. The authority that Christ possesses is absolute. As Head of the Church He has delegated authority to His body:

1. **Over sickness and demons**

   He ... gave them authority to drive out evil spirits and to heal every disease and sickness. (Matthew 10:1)

2. **Over all of Satan's power**

   'I have given you authority to trample on snakes and scorpions and to overcome all the power of the enemy; nothing will harm you.' (Luke 10:19)

3. **Over circumstances**

   '... whatever you bind on earth will be bound in heaven, and whatever you loose on earth will be loosed in heaven.' (Matthew 18:18)

How do we know what authority to exercise and when to exercise it? That is the crucial question – and one that is mostly overlooked in teaching on the authority of the believer. An impression can be given that because we have authority over all the power of Satan, we can just go out and, of our own volition, put to rights everything that we think is wrong. That of course is nonsense.

If I am faced with difficult circumstances there are always a number of possible explanations. It may be due to my own mistake, or sin; it may be something that God has allowed to teach me to overcome it; it may be something that God wants me to go through; or it may be something that the enemy has organized in order to attack me. Only in some of these situations can I exercise authority to change the situation. If, for example, God wants to teach me something by going through difficult circumstances, He will not supply the power to change the circumstances – even if I try to exercise authority over them.

Jesus knew, even on the cross, that He had authority to call twelve legions of angels to His aid. He did not use that authority because He had in view a greater authority: the authority He would gain, through His death and resurrection, to give to us the right to become sons of God.

The answer to the use of authority is that:

▶   **We know when to exercise authority and how to exercise it by the prompting of the Holy Spirit discerned in our conscience**.

There is an example in the thirteenth chapter of Acts, when Elymas the magician opposed Paul's preaching and tried to turn the proconsul Sergius Paulus from the faith. What did Paul do? He did not argue with Elymas, as he was well able to do, but he responded to the prompting of the Spirit upon him.

> *Then Saul, who was also called Paul, filled with the Holy Spirit, looked straight at Elymas and said, 'You are a child of the devil and an enemy of everything that is right! You are full of all kinds of deceit and trickery. Will you never stop perverting the right ways of the Lord? Now the hand of the Lord is against you. You are going to be blind, and for a time you will be unable to see the light of the sun.' Immediately mist and darkness came over him, and he groped about, seeking someone to lead him by the hand. When the proconsul saw what had happened, he believed, for he was amazed at the teaching about the Lord.*   (Acts 13:9–12)

In Acts chapter 9, Peter came to the saints at Lydda and found there Aeneas, who had been bed-ridden for eight years because he was paralyzed. Peter did not pray for Aeneas to be healed – probably the saints had often done so – he healed him.

> *'Aeneas', Peter said to him, 'Jesus Christ heals you. Get up and tidy up your mat.' Immediately Aeneas got up. All those*

> who lived in Lydda and Sharon saw him and turned to the
> Lord.   (Acts 9:34–35)

Such authority, with the release of power that produces
results, can only come about when exercised in prompt and
humble obedience to the direction of the Holy Spirit.

The means are obedience and authority – and both are
necessary. If we are not living in obedience, we can
command as loud as we like and as long as we like: nothing
will happen because no power will enforce the word. On the
other hand, if we do not exercise the authority that has been
delegated to us, nothing will happen: not because there is no
power to back us up, but because it has not been brought to
bear on the situation. It is when both links operate that the
power of the Holy Spirit is released to heal and deliver, to
bind and loose, and to change and overrule circumstances
and situations.

The spiritual nature of authority

There is a very important aspect of the whole subject of
authority that is generally overlooked, but is clearly illustrated in Figure 22 (page 222). That is,

▶ **True authority is always spiritual in origin.**

Because of this, it functions from the spirit of the person
exercising it and it reaches the spirit of the person over
whom it is being exercised. Therefore, it will affect the latter
person in his conscience: there will be an 'oughtness' about
the order or instruction. Nevertheless, the person's will is left
free to obey or disobey. Obedience is therefore a free choice
and has the liberating effect of all true obedience.

If, however, the person exercising authority is not himself
living in obedience, what comes out from him is not spiritual
authority but soul power. Cover up obedience in the diagram
in Figure 23 (page 221) and you will see that what emerges no
longer has its source in the spirit but in the soul. What will
come out is most often willpower; but there may also be
strong emotional pressure or forceful argument. Because it is

grounded in the soul, it will touch the other person in his soul. There will be a clash of wills, a conflict of argument or opposing feelings. The person who is being given the orders or instructions will either give way to superior power (but feel resentful and rebellious at the same time), or he will 'stand up for himself' and there will be open conflict.

When I obey true authority, I do not feel inferior or diminished, because true authority is spiritual and respects my moral freedom. Authority that is not legitimate (but is the imposition of another's will or ideas) does not respect my moral freedom. It seeks to coerce or manipulate – and I either conform or rebel. I am usually in less danger by rebelling.

It is crucial for parents to understand this principle – and equally important for church leadership. As Menno Simon said over four hundred years ago, spiritual authority in the Church is never to make the rebel conform, it is to enable the obedient person to live a holy life.

Expectancy and joy

One of the features of the charismatic renewal around the world, is the return of joy to the people of God. Helmut Thelieke, the great German preacher, wrote that Christians coming out of church on Sunday mornings, instead of looking as though they had been at the Father's banquet, usually looked as if they had just had their sins auctioned off – and were wishing that they had them back! Praise God that there are many gatherings of the saints today in which such a conclusion would be impossible.

Creation itself was born in joy. When the foundations of the earth were laid, the book of Job tells us, '... *the morning stars sang together and all the angels shouted for joy*' (Job 38:7).

Again, in the great Old Testament passage on Christ as Wisdom we read:

> ... *when he marked out the foundations of the earth. Then I was the craftsman at his side. I was filled with delight day after day, rejoicing always in his presence, rejoicing in his whole world and delighting in mankind.*   (Proverbs 8:29–31)

Human beings have a created need to experience joy; a need for ecstasy would not be putting it too strongly! We hunger in our heart to know transcendent joy. Ever since Eve saw in the tree of the knowledge of good and evil the promise of delight, human beings have sought such experiences. Today they seek them through sex, mind-expanding drugs, occult mysticism, meditation techniques and so on. Some of these ways are both harmful and dangerous, others may be more positive; but all are non-Christian, and therefore ultimately fail to produce lasting results.

There are two things we need to know about the search for joy. The first is that **joy is always a by-product**. It can never be an object or an end in itself. It is always, when genuine, the by-product of another experience. To seek joy as joy, like seeking happiness for happiness' sake, immediately guarantees that we will not find it. The search is, in fact, counterproductive. You can become more miserable seeking joy than before you began.

The second is the nature of the experience of which joy is the by-product. The Bible reveals quite clearly that for human beings, transcendent joy comes from one experience alone: **the experience of personal encounter with the living God.**

> *Then will I go to the altar of God,*
> *to God, my joy and delight.*   (Psalm 43:4)

> *...you will fill me with joy in your presence,*
> *with eternal pleasures at your right hand.*   (Psalm 16:11)

> *...the kingdom of God is not a matter of eating and drinking, but of righteousness, peace and joy in the Holy Spirit.*   (Romans 14:17)

> *Though you have not seen him, you love him; and even though you do not see him now, you believe in him and are filled with an inexpressible and glorious joy...*   (1 Peter 1:8)

It was this last verse that first made me realize that if the words meant what they seemed to mean, then after a quarter of a century of Christian experience I had clearly missed something very vital. I could not even imagine what it meant to be *'filled with an inexpressible and glorious joy'*!

I will never forget the night that I was baptized in the Holy Spirit. By that time I had it all worked out as to what was likely to happen, because I had been reading a lot of books on revival. I concluded that if God really met me, as I longed He would, He would convict me to the soles of my feet regarding my exceeding sinfulness. I cranked up my courage for just such a thing because I was desperate for reality.

But what happened was totally different from all my expectations. In the depth of my spirit, as I was being prayed for, I touched God the Holy Spirit and there burst up from within me a gushing of pure, ineffable joy. After all my doubts and fears I found that God was real, He was wonderful, and He was within me. I laughed for joy, I shouted for joy. In the end I had to tell the Lord to stop. I had more than I could manage for a time! Oh, hallelujah! The wonderful thing is, that after over twenty years, the experience is as fresh and new and exciting and joyful today as it ever was – and more so.

Now, can you see the link between hope and joy? The expectancy that enables us to experience the presence of the Holy Spirit finds its fulfillment in joy.

> *May the God of hope fill you with all joy and peace as you trust in him...* (Romans 15:13)

The fruit of the Holy Spirit begins in joy. The early disciples, we read, were *'filled with joy and with the Holy Spirit'* (Acts 13:52).

In the body the negative emotions, like fear and resentment, can cause functional and ultimately organic disturbances, but joy is therapeutic. It is life-giving.

> *A happy heart makes the face cheerful,*
> *but heartache crushes the spirit.* (Proverbs 15:13)

> *A cheerful heart is good medicine,*
> *but a crushed spirit dries up the bones.* (Proverbs 17:22)

Let me hear joy and gladness;
  let the bones you have crushed rejoice.   (Psalm 51:8)

Do not grieve, for the joy of the Lord is your strength.
                                        (Nehemiah 8:10)

It is recorded of one of John Wesley's old preachers, that when he came to his deathbed, 'his joy at the prospect of seeing his Savior face to face was so extreme, it kept him alive for another fortnight.' I love that! Can't you imagine the old warrior, ecstatic with joy because at last he was going to see Jesus? And the joy causes adrenaline to pump through his frail old body, keeping him alive day after day.

Finally, joy, by its very nature, has to be expressed. It is very important to see how much joy there is in Scripture. Take any concordance and look at the number of times words like joy, rejoice, and gladness appear, and see with what they are linked: singing (Psalm 71:23), shouting (Isaiah 35:10), dancing (Jeremiah 31:13), leaping (Luke 6:23), clapping hands (Psalm 47:1), music (1 Chronicles 15:28), and so on.

Joy is the secret of real evangelism, for joyful Christians are a compelling advertisement for the gospel. Joy in the Holy Spirit is unquenchable and independent of circumstances, because it can neither be produced by them, nor taken away by them. Jesus said to the disciples, '. . . *I will see you again and you will rejoice, and no one will take away your joy'* (John 16:22).

In our human spirit there dwells the source of joy: God the Holy Spirit. When we live in an attitude of open expectancy (or hope) towards Him, then joy will be our portion. With joy we will continually draw water from the wells of salvation.

If you have enjoyed this book and would like to help us to send a copy of it and many other titles to needy pastors in the **Third World**, please write for further information or send your gift to:

Sovereign World Trust
PO Box 777, Tonbridge
Kent TN11 0ZS
United Kingdom

or to the **'Sovereign World'** distributor in your country.

Visit our website at **www.sovereign-world.org**
for a full range of Sovereign World books.